Aboriginal Mythology

Aboriginal Mythology

*An A–Z spanning the history of
aboriginal mythology from the
earliest legends to the present day*

Mudrooroo

Thorsons
An Imprint of HarperCollins*Publishers*

Thorsons
An Imprint of HarperCollins*Publishers*
77–85 Fulham Palace Road,
Hammersmith, London W6 8JB

Published by Aquarian 1994
3   5   7   9   10   8   6   4

A catalogue record for this book
is available from the British Library

ISBN 1 85538 306 3

Printed in Great Britain by
HarperCollinsManufacturing Glasgow

Contents

Introduction

There are over 300,000 Australian Aborigine people, divided into many clans, language groups and local communities. They are related by kin ties, either biological or classificatory. Kinship was and is the tie which binds the communities, not only to each other, but to the stars above and the earth below and the plants, the animals, the very rocks and landscape. To the Aboriginal person, the entire universe is permeated with life—it is a living, breathing biomass which has separated into families. There are families of stars, of trees and of animals, and these are connected to our human families. Our way of life is spiritual in that there is an interconnectedness, an interrelatedness with all existence, existence extending from the merely physical realms to the spiritual, encapsulated in the term 'the Dreaming'. The Dreaming is a continuous process of creation which began in the long ago period called the 'Dreamtime', when the physical features of the land were formed by creative beings who were neither human or animal, but had the attributes of both. It was through the actions of these primordial ancestors that flora and fauna, including humanity, evolved. It was

also from this time and from these ancestors that rites and ceremonies came into being. Sacred places were formed, where certain
actions occurred and where the ancestors left part of their energy
(*djang*), which may be actualized in the present through rites and
ceremonies to ensure that the species of creation remain abun-
dant.

The ancestors also set in place the often complicated and formal
kinship system, to which all the species of creation belong. This
order has survived in many Aboriginal communities to this day. It
was and is never exclusive, so outsiders may be adopted into the
structure and given a place and a family designation which impose
obligations as a family member. Thus, before the coming of the
British, Indonesian persons who visited the northern shores of
Australia were taken into the kinship system. When the British
settlers came, those who established friendly relations were also
taken into the family groups. It is because of this non-exclusivity
that the blood which flows through our veins is a mixture of Malay,
Chinese, European and any others who have been taken into our
kinship system.

Aboriginal people believe that they have lived in Australia from
the beginning of all things and archaeologists have dated the
human occupancy of Australia back many tens of thousands of
years to the time when Australia was part of a huge mass of land
connected with New Guinea and parts of Asia. This has been
named Gondwanaland and identified with the ancient legendary
continent of Mu. So it may be said that the Aboriginal people's
occupancy of this great south land really does extend back to the
Dreamtime.

The culture and physique of the Australian Aborigines reflect
the environment of Australia with its many climates and terrains,
the stark beauty of its deserts and the overabundance of its rainforests. An Aboriginal population map of Australia shows the
people spread across the land in small bands of hunters and gath-
erers, moving with the seasons or when necessity demanded and
remaining stationary for long periods when food was plentiful. The
people can be roughly divided into two groups: sea people, those
who relied on the waters and coastline for their sustenance; and
land people, those who inhabited areas away from the coasts and
lived off the resources of the land. This division is also found in the
mythology. Among coastal people there are stories of cultural
heroes arriving from across the sea bringing new ways of thought,
while among the land people ancestral and cultural heroes come
from the land and either return to the land or ascend into the
skies. A common trait of such ancestral and cultural heroes is the
journeys they undertake, some for incredible distances, and this

on foot, or under the earth, or through the air.

Each community, clan or family group owned its own estate, large or small depending on the climate and environment. It was believed that their estate had been given to them at the very beginning of time, when the ancestors created the landscape and established the laws and customs which governed family and inter-family relationships.

Not only had the land, the laws and customs been given to the different families, but also their languages. There were once hundreds of different languages and dialects, and many people were multi-lingual, for each language, having been given to the individual family groups by the ancestors, had to be maintained by their descendants. Marriage laws played a large part in making Aborigines multi-lingual. Marriage was exogamous and women went to live with the family of the groom, who often spoke a different language. There was and still is a reciprocity between different family groups and marriage was important in maintaining and strengthening this, especially in regard to hunting and food-gathering rights. Reciprocity networks extended across Australia and, although on occasion there were family squabbles, ceremonies such as the Rom and Fire ceremony sought to regulate the peace. Because of the huge size of Australia, however, to speak of a unified Aboriginal race is wrong to say the least. As the land, the climate, the environment varied, so did the various families living on their estates.

History was slow and even for thousands of years, though the coming and going of the ice age from 10,000 to 6,000 years ago must have resulted in as much change to the Aboriginal population as it did to the climate and the environment. In 1788, there occurred an event of momentous importance to all Aboriginal people: a party of British soldiers and convicts under the command of Governor Phillip landed in the country of the Eora people. This first landing was followed by others at various places along the coast, and the landings turned into a veritable invasion as Aboriginal family groups found themselves deprived of their land and even shot if they tried to defend their land rights. Bloodshed and turmoil followed, with the Aboriginal population being drastically thinned out, especially along the eastern coast-line, where the survivors found themselves strangers in their own land. Missionaries came to 'civilize' us. We were forbidden to speak our own languages and were collected together into reserves and missions. We were massacred and murdered everywhere and the marks of that 200-odd year history are still with us. It is only now that we are seeking self-determination for ourselves and trying to protect and revitalize our languages, culture and way of life against those who still rule us.

Many Aboriginal groups are very conservative in that they believe that laws and customs passed down from the ancestors are the best which can be followed. They are slow to accept change and if they do so, these changes must be accommodated to the belief systems passed down through the ages: what was good for the ancestors was and is good for their descendants. Thus the hunting and gathering way of life persists to this day, especially in northern and central Australia, where the British had little impact. Along the northern coastlines before the coming of the British, the Aboriginal people of Cape York traded with the Melanesian people living in the Torres Strait and New Guinea. The Melanesians planted crops and tended gardens, used bows and arrows and beat on drums. The northern Aboriginal people took the bow and arrow and the drum into their ceremonies, but made no other use of them, for the hunting and gathering system worked well. In other places and among other groups, however, this way of life was quickly put an end to when our lands were taken from us.

The invasion by the British resulted in the greatest catastrophe for many Aboriginal groups since the end of the ice age and the rising of the seas. The British, unlike the earlier Malay visitors, were a non-traditional people who came to stay. They disregarded all of the Aboriginal customs and beliefs, took the land and dis-possessed the Aboriginal land-owning groups whenever and wher-ever they wanted. It was a cruel time, a killing time. Diseases were introduced which swept the land and the remnants of our people were herded into reserves. Many died, especially in the southern temperate parts, and the stunned survivors became 'wards of the state' and were given rations of flour, sugar and tea, and allowed to eke out a miserable existence. Christian missionaries came to help us, and decided that our ceremonies, our beliefs, our rites and rituals were the work of the devil. We reeled under the onslaught, though many of us remained true to our ancestors, but it was a time of great change, great calamity, and many of our customs, languages and oral records were lost, or changed when they were written down. It is only now that we are recovering from those killing times.

Still, in our collective lives, the last 200 years is but a brief spell, a wink of an eye, and whereas the British and other invaders live from day to day, from year to year, we live from epoch to epoch. Our rich oral historical tradition reaches back to the ice age and even beyond to when the giant marsupials roamed Australia. Not only this, but our culture is considered to be one of the oldest in the world, with some of our rock art being accepted as the first known examples of human art. We still paint, we still dance, we still tell our stories, we still sing our songs, and some of our beliefs and stories are recorded in this volume. Perhaps our essential belief is that we belong to this land of Australia, that it is our mother or father and that we must care for her or him. That it was given to us of old and that no one can take it away. As Bill Neidjie, a traditional owner of Kakadu National Park, declares in his book, *Story about Feeling*:

Ground...
We hang on.
This earth for us.
Just like mother, father, sister.

Thus many, if not most, of our stories and myths are land-centred, and reflect that interconnectedness with all of existence, that reciprocity between all, that should not be lost. The universe is a biomass and we must tend it, for we are the caretakers, and we are not lost souls, but parts of a whole in which everything is related. So we should not pillage and destroy, but co-operate and tolerate, nurture and care for the whole universe with its myriads of living and breathing things.

The continent of Australia is vast and such was the distance, such was the number of Aboriginal family groups, that customs and languages, stories and records, vary from place to place. There are long dialect chains of language and over the links changes occur, so much so that a word may reverse its meaning by the time the end of the dialect chain is reached. As for language, so it is for our customs and myths. Long myth song circles and stories travel over the land, ordering and shaping it, naming and renaming things and landmarks. Some of these myths and stories are found in this volume.

In a book of Australian Aboriginal mythology it is difficult not to risk offending some groups in that secret sacred material may have been inadvertently used. An apology is given here if there is any revealing of things that should not be revealed. Care should be taken in using this book when Aboriginal people are present and an elder should be asked to check it out. Again, in some Aboriginal communities there is a prohibition in the use of a person's name after death. This prohibition is of varying lengths of time and I have tried to name only deceased persons after the time of mourning has passed. It is a little difficult to keep to this sanction, as it is not a universal custom and whilst I was writing this book some of our elders and relatives died. This volume is dedicated to them. I have sat around the campfire in dry, dusty places and in clearings in rain forests listening to our story-tellers. It is as much their book as it is mine. I trust I have kept to a promise I made to tell their stories so that everyone can understand a little of our culture and way of life. I near the end of this introduction with a few words from Bill Neidjie, whom I met some years ago in his country, now called Kakadu National Park:

You listen my story and you will feel im
Because spirit e'll be with you
You cannot see but e'll be with you e'll be with me
This story just listen careful.

Please note that the spelling of Aboriginal words varies quite markedly. I have tried to give the variations which are known to me. In regard to the people I have named, in Aboriginal culture, the first name is usually used and I have kept to this practice in my book, though deleting the kin term which usually precedes it.

A

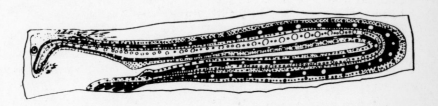

The Great Ancestral Being of the Nyungar

Aboriginal and Aborigine The words 'Aboriginal' and 'Aborigine' are used by the invaders to designate the indigenous people of Australia. They are seldom used by indigenous people themselves, who prefer their own words. These often simply mean 'people', such as *Koori* (south-east Australia), *Nyungar* (south-west Australia), *Nanga* (South Australia), Wonghi (*Western Desert*), Yolngu (*Arnhem Land*), Murri (south Queensland) and *Yamadji* (Pilbara region of Western Australia). There is no Australia-wide indigenous word for the whole people, so Aboriginal and Aborigine remain in use until such a word can be found and generally accepted.

Adno-artina the gecko lizard See *Parachilna; Red ochre.*

Adnyamathanha people The Adnyamathanha people are the traditional owners of the *Flinders Range* in South Australia. Although much of their traditional culture has been lost, or been changed drastically in response to the British invasion, a tribal revitalization programme centred on Nepabunna Aboriginal School began in 1984. The Adnyamathanha language (*Yuru Ngawarla*) and culture are being taught and in 1986 young Adnyamathanha people met at the *Aboriginal* keeping-place, Pichi Richi, in Alice Springs in central Australia, to learn about their *Dreaming* and associated stories.

The Adnyamathanha people are symbolized by the iga, the native orange tree (*Capparis mitchellii*). It is related by the *elders* that in the *Dreaming* the iga tree was a man who came from Yaramangga in Queensland. He gained a wife on his travels and engaged in battle with the mulga trees. Eventually, they settled in the Flinders Range and became the ancestors of the Adnyamathanha people.

Akngwelye See *Arrernte landscape of Alice Springs*.

Akurra serpent The Akurra serpent deity of the *Adnyamathanha people* belongs to the great corpus of snake mythology which extends across Australia. The serpent is sometimes known as the *rainbow snake* or serpent and the Adnyamathanha Akurra serpent is similar to our *Nyungar* creative ancestor, the *Wagyal*. Adnyamathanha *elders* describe it as a huge water snake with a beard, mane, scales and very sharp fangs. The Wagyal has been described to me as being a huge water snake, *black* in colour, with a hairy neck. In the *Flinders Range*, as in south-western Australia, the marks of Akurra's passing are found all across the land. As with other serpents, Akurra is associated with the power of the *shamans*. Only they may go near him with impunity.

As in many other cultures, serpents are associated with water and rain. This association is brought out in the Adnyamathanha story:

Once the people were suffering from lack of food caused by a prolonged drought. They travelled to a cave in which the Akurra serpent lived and the shamans got Akurra out from his cave. They took his kidney fat and heated it to make rain by holding it over a fire and letting the melted fat fall onto the coals. A strong wind arose as the smell of the burning fat ascended into the sky. Rain clouds gathered and burst. Down came showers of rain. The creeks flooded and plant foods sprang up everywhere.

See also *Rain-making*.

Albert, Stephen See *Baamba*.

Aldebaran Aldebaran, a double star in the constellation Taurus, symbolized Gallerlek the rose-crested cockatoo for the *Koori* people of Victoria. In their myth he chased the female *Pleiades* when on *Earth* and followed them into the sky. Versions of this myth are found all across Australia, with the pursuer and the women identified with different beings.

Alice Springs See *Adnyamathanha people; Arrernte landscape of Alice Springs; Arrernte people; Hermannsburg Mission; Molonga ceremonies*.

Alinda See *Death*.

All-Fathers The All-Fathers, or the Great Father deities, form the basis of mythology in a number of *Aboriginal* communities and perhaps are a result of the influence of Christianity. They are primordial deities who are said to have come before the ancestors, although often the *rainbow snake* may be seen as the All-Father (or All-Mother) deity in the sense that all things stem from him or her.

All-Father deities have a number of features in common, for example each sent sons to *Earth* to carry out designs for humankind, to care for them and to punish evil doers. Some of these All-Father deities are: *Biame*, widely known throughout south-eastern Australia, and his son Daramulun (or Gayandi); Nooralie of the *Murray river* area and his son Gnawdenoorte; Mungan Ngour of the Kurnai *community* and his son Tundun.

See also *All-Mothers; Creation myths*.

All-Mothers The All-Mothers are similar to the All-Father deities and are often their wives or some of their wives. The most important All-Mother is Birrahgnooloo, the chief wife of *Biame*. Gunabibi (or Kunapipi) is another important All-Mother, whose worship is extensive in northern Australia (see *Gunabibi ceremonies*); another is *Warramurrauungi*. The great snake or *rainbow snake* is often seen as the mother of all things, though perhaps it should be seen to be androgynous.

See also *All-Fathers; Creation myths; Gunabibi; Gunabibi*

ceremonies; Mudungkala.

Altair For the *Koori* people of Victoria, Altair, a star in the constellation Aquila, represented *Bunjil*, Eaglehawk, the *moiety ancestor* who, it seems, evolved into an All-Father deity under the influence of Christianity. The stars to each side of him were his two wives, the *black* swans.

Among the people of the *Murray river*, Altair was Totyerguil, the son of Neil-loan (Lyra), and the stars on either side were his two wives. He was killed when his mother-in-law made him fall into a waterhole. His body was recovered by Collenbitjik (the double star in *Capricornus*), who was his mother's brother.

Altjeringa See *Dreamtime*.

Ancestral beings Ancestral beings are considered to be those *Dreamtime* beings who shaped the world and eventually transformed into human beings, the fauna and flora that we find today. They are the great archetypes of existence and can be contacted through dreams and ceremonies.

The Great Ancestral Being of the *Nyungar* people is considered to be the *Wagyal*, a primordial snake deity who formed everything and who is still with us.

See also *All-Fathers; All-Mothers; Bandicoot ancestor; Creation myths; Dreamtime; Djanggawul and his two sisters myth; Dogs; Dreamtime; Wandjina; Walbiri creation myth; Walkabout; Women ancestral beings.*

Animal behaviour Animals behaving in an unusual manner were considered by many *Aboriginal* communities to be the spirits of the dead or simply spirits who had possessed animal bodies in order to get close to human beings in order to harm them, though there were also friendly spirits who came in the guise of animals to warn humans of danger. These generally took the form of *Dreaming* (totem or moiety) animals. There are many stories of ghosts in the guise of animals.

It was widely believed that *shamans* could turn into animals, for example *Paddy Roe*, an elder and story-teller of the Broome area of Western Australia, relates the story of the shaman Mirdinan who escaped from prison by turning first into a cat, then an eaglehawk.

Antares Antares, in the constellation Scorpius, to the Wotjobaluk *Kooris* of Victoria represented Djuit, son of Marpean-kurrk (*Arcturus*), and the stars on either side were his wives.

To the Kulin Kooris, Antares was *Balayang, Bunjil*'s brother. See also *Totems*.

Aragwal See *Bundjalung nation*.

Aranda people See *Arrernte people*.

Arcturus Arcturus, the brightest star in the constellation *Bootes*, to the *Koori* people was Marpean-kurrk, mother of Djuit (*Antares*) and Weet-kurrk (a star in Bootes). Marpean-kurrk was the ancestral being who introduced the larvae of the wood-ant as a food. During August and September, when they were in season for the Kooris, they were out of season for her and she was not visible in the sky. When Arcturus was in the north in the evening, the larvae were coming into season. When the star set with the *sun* (in the west), the larvae were finished and summer had begun.

Arnhem Land Arnhem Land in the far north of Australia is the home of the Yolngu people. Much of it was once a government reserve for *Aboriginal* people and, as it was away from the main areas of British influence, the Aboriginal culture there maintained strong links with tradition. Since the Northern Territory Land Rights Act of 1976, much of the reserve has reverted to Aboriginal control.

See also *Barama and Laindjung myths; Bark paintings; Black; Bralgu; Death; Dhambidj song series of Arnhem Land; Djanggawul mythology and ceremonies; Djanggawul and his two sisters myth; Duwa moiety; Fire; Great Mother; Ground carvings and sculptures; Gunabibi; Hollow log coffins; Honey; Luma Luma the giant; Marwai; Mimi spirits; Morning Star song series; Nara; North-eastern Arnhem Land; Red ochre; Rom ceremony of Arnhem Land; Thunder Man; Wangarr; Yellow ochre; Yiritja; Yothu Yindi; Yuendumu.*

Arrernte landscape of Alice Springs Alice Springs in central Australia in the country of the Mparntwe group of the *Arrernte people* is an example of how the *Aboriginal* landscape of Australia continues to endure under the buildings of a modern city.

Alice Springs is situated on a flat area surrounded by bluffs, two of which are Anzac Hill and Annie Meyer Hill. From the top of

Anzac Hill to the south the Todd river passes through the city area to Ntaripe (Heavitree Gap), while eastwards there is a dip in the Heavitree Range called Anthwerrke (Emily Gap). This is the sacred *djang* place where the caterpillar ancestors of Mparntwe originated. It was they who formed the landscape around Alice Springs. There were three species of caterpillar, Yepereny, Ntyarika and Utnerrengatyre, which can still be found, though because of the city enclosing their *djang* sites, the increase ceremonies to keep up their numbers have been abandoned. The caterpillar ancestors came from Anthwerrke and created the small ridge, Ntyarlkarle Tyaneme, behind the Desert Palms Motel. Unfortunately, this sacred ridge has been desecrated by the municipal authorities and the road, Barrett Drive, has been renamed Broken Promise Drive by the Arrernte people of Mparntwe to remind them of what happens when the sacred gets in the way of progress.

Ntaripe has other sacred sites, including one sacred to the Dog ancestor, here called Akngwelye, who formed most of the features of the Mt Gillen range. The Dog fought a major battle here before transforming into a boulder embedded in the ground near Akeyulerre (Billy Goat Hill). This boulder now sits outside the entrance to a fast food outlet.

Within the Olive Pink Flora Reserve, towards the south-eastern end of the hill, near Lhere Mparntwe (Todd river), is a sign indicating the location of several Arrernte sacred places. The Arrernte people are striving to protect them in the face of determined opposition from those who wish to exploit the area for tourism. The traditional owner of the area, Thomas Stevens, has written a book about the effects of British colonization on his country called *Damaging our Dreaming Land*, published by the Yipirinya School Literacy Production Centre in central Australia.

See also *Arrernte people*.

Arrernte people The Arrernte (Aranda or Arunta) people are a large *community* speaking a number of dialects whose country is centred about Alice Springs in central Australia. The western Arrernte groups were concentrated in the *Hermannsburg Mission*, which was founded in 1877 by German missionaries. Although they fostered the use of the Arrernte language, they were against Arrernte spirituality and exorcized the main keeping-place of sacred objects (*tjuringa*) at Manangananga cave, two kilometres north of the mission, in 1928. They conducted a Christian ceremony at this sacred place, which until then was forbidden to all but initiated men. This resulted in the disintegration for some time of Arrernte spirituality. *Tjuringa* were sold to tourists and sacred songs to anthropologists at a shilling a time. In the mid-1950s, however, there occurred a tribal revitalization movement which saw the resacralization of Manangananga cave. The *elders* of the Arrernte considered the devastating scurvy epidemic which swept the mission in 1929 to be the result of the earlier sacrilege. By the 1970s the sale of *tjuringa* and songs was at an end.

See also *Arrernte landscape of Alice Springs*.

Arta-wararlpanha (Mount Serle) Arta-wararlpanha in the *Flinders Range* is a sacred place of the *Adnyamathanha people*. In the *Dreamtime* it is said that it was created by two snakes. Two rocky points are said to be their heads. Arta-wararlpanha was one of the last areas of the Adnyamathanha people to hold out against the invaders and the ritual masters who led the resistance at the turn of the nineteenth century are buried there.

Arunta people See *Arrernte people*.

Assimilation policy The assimilation policy was formulated by the government in the 1930s to forcibly integrate *Aboriginal* people into the mainstream society of Australia. In order to do this, children were taken away from their parents and placed in institutions. This policy made many *Aborigines* alien to their own culture and traditions and it has only been since 1967, when the policy was officially abandoned, that the persons belonging to what we call 'the stolen generations' have been relinking to their heritage without government interference.

See also *Namatjira, Albert; Papunya*.

Aurora Australis The Aurora Australis, or Southern Lights, according to the Kurnai *Koori* people of Victoria, is a sign of anger from the All-Father Mungan Ngour. A myth explains why. When Mungan Ngour laid down the rules for the initiation of boys into manhood, he placed his son Tundun in charge of the secret men's ceremonies. Someone divulged them to the women and Mungan Ngour became angry and a time of great chaos ensured in which people ran amok, killing one another, and the seas rushed in, flooding much of the land. This ended the *Dreaming* period and after this Tundun and his wife became porpoises. The All-Father ascended into the sky, and if his laws and customs are disregarded he shows his anger by lighting up the sky at night.

Australian indigenous mythology Australian indigenous mythology serves many purposes and is land and people based. The mythology is encoded in stories which are handed down and if the stories are detached from the land and people, then the story is being changed to reflect other concerns.

The indigenous mythology gives the history of important places. The stories account for the origins of natural phenomena: they relate how natural features of the landscape were created; how species were created; the origins of stars, mountains, rocky outcrops, *waterholes* and minerals. Mythology accounts for things as they are. The mythological stories are also maps—it is through story, song and sacred objects (*tjuringa*) that the country of a people or *community* is mapped and the boundaries kept in mind. Mythology is also a way of passing geographical knowledge from generation to generation, thus where the thumping kangaroo first thumped there is limestone; the goanna is associated with sandy outcrops; the kingfisher with coal; the pigeon with gold; and the crested pigeon with grinding stones. It must be emphasized that often when we talk of animals, we are also referring back to the *Dreaming* ancestor from which they evolved and which they still symbolize. It is from such Dreaming ancestors that all the laws and the social organization of particular communities come. It is when this connection is lost that these stories become simple tales—'How the echidna got its spikes' and so on. The mythology encoded in the stories is much more important that this.

Stories record the boundaries of tribal countries, and when the story or song line stops, that is the boundary. It is not that the travels of the Dreaming ancestors stopped, but that another community has custodianship of the next section of the journey and thus ownership of a particular tract of country.

Stories also contain blueprints for special rituals: for *rainmaking*, saving sick children from *death*, the customs for widowhood, initiation and so on and so forth. Without the mythological sanction of a story or a corpus of stories and *song lines*, customs and laws have no legality. Where *Aboriginal* traditional culture is upheld and the stories known by the community, they provide guidelines for living. They focus on social relationships and moral values and their preservation for social well-being: what was done in the Dreaming by the ancestors is to be done now. Mythology also embodies warnings for those who break the rules, gives courage in times of adversity and is a focus of community identity. A particular community has its own corpus of stories and these give social cohesion and identity. When these stories and songs extend beyond the particular community, such as the great myth circles like the Seven Sisters, the *Two Men* and the Melatji *dogs*, they unite all those communities having the same Dreaming ancestors or cultural heroes. This intertribal or intercommunity identification is stressed at the important ceremonies, such as the man-making ceremonies in which many separate communities participate.

Australites Australites are small stones which have fallen from the *sky world* and thus have magical healing properties which are utilized by *shamans* for curing aches and pains such as toothache. It is said that if they are thrown into running water, they will return to their homes, the place where they were found.

Auwa *Auwa* is the *Wik Munggan* people's name for a *djang* or *sacred place*.

Aversion countries See *Taboo countries*.

Awabakal people The Awabakal people owned the area around the town of Newcastle in New South Wales. As with many of the peoples along the eastern seaboard, their culture has been drastically modernized, with many of the old traditions changing to accommodate the way of life which came in with the invasion, through tribal revitalization movements keep aspects of the ancient customs alive.

Ayer's Rock See *Uluru*.

B

Bull-roarers

Baamba Baamba (Stephen Albert) is a story-teller and singer from the Broome area. He has also acted in *Bran Nue Dae*, an *Aboriginal* musical which has played to packed houses throughout Australia.

Badurra See *Ground carvings and sculptures*.

Baiame See *Biame*.

Balayang Balayang bat mythology exists only in fragments and much has been lost. To the Kulin people of Victoria Balayang the bat was a brother to the great *Bunjil* the eaglehawk, but lived apart from him. Once, Bunjil asked him to come to where he was living, for it was a much better country, but Balayang replied that it was too dry and that Bunjil should come to where *he* was living. This upset Bunjil, so he sent his two helpers, Djurt-djurt the nankeen kestral and Thara the quail hawk, to Balayang. They set *fire* to his country and Balayang and his children were scorched and turned *black*.

Because of his black colour, Balayang was associated with *Crow* and thus belonged to the moiety in opposition to Eaglehawk. This is in keeping with another story about Balayang which credits him with creating or finding women—and thus marriage partners—for the Eaglehawk moiety. One day Balayang was amusing himself with thumping the surface of the water and he thumped away until it thickened into mud. Something stirred and he took a bough and probed the mud. Presently he saw four hands, two heads, then two bodies. It was two women. He called one Kunnawarra, Black Swan, and the other Kururuk, Native Companion. He took them to Bunjil, who gave them as wives to the men he had created.

To the Kulin people, *Antares* symbolized Balayang.

See also *Eaglehawk and Crow*.

Balin the barramundi See *Milky Way*.

Balin-ga the porcupine See *Great corroborees*.

Balugaan See *Dogs; Tooloom Falls*.

Balur See *Barrier Reef*.

Banbai See *Bundjalung nation*.

Bandicoot ancestor The bandicoot ancestor myth is found among the Arrernte *community*. In the *Dreamtime* everywhere was darkness and the bandicoot ancestor, Karora, was lying in the earth asleep; then from him sprang a tall pole, called a *tnatantja*. Its bottom rested on his head and its top rose up into the sky. It was a living creature covered with a smooth skin.

Karora began thinking and from his armpits and navel burst forth bandicoots who dug themselves out from the earth just as the first *sun* spread light across the sky. Karora followed them. He seized two young bandicoots, cooked them and ate them. Satisfied, he laid down to sleep and while he slept from under his armpit emerged a *bull-roarer*. It took on human form and grew into a young man. Karora awoke and his son danced about his father. It was the very first ceremony. The son hunted for bandicoots and they cooked and ate them. Karora slept and whilst sleeping created two more sons. This went on for some time and he created many more sons. They ate up all the bandicoots which originally came forth from their father and became hungry. They hunted far and wide but could find no game. On the way back, they heard the sound of a bull-roarer. They searched for the man who might be swinging it. Suddenly something darted up from their feet and they called, 'There goes a sandhill wallaby!' They hurled their *tjuringa* sticks at it and broke its leg. The sandhill wallaby sang out that he was now lame and was a man like them, not a bandicoot. He then limped away.

The hunters continued on their way and saw their father approaching. He led them back to the waterhole. They sat on the edge of the pool and then from the east came a great flood of honey from the honeysuckle buds and engulfed them. The father remained at the soak, but his sons were swirled away to where sandhill wallaby man they had lamed waited for them. The spot became a great *djang* place and there the rocks which are the brothers are still grouped around a boulder which is said to be the body of the sandhill wallaby man.

At the sacred waterhole where Karora is said to be lying in eternal sleep, those who come to drink from it must carry green boughs which they lay down on the banks before easing their thirst. It is said that Karora is pleased with this and smiles in his sleep.

Barama and Laindjung myths The Barama and Laindjung myths from *Arnhem Land* are *Yiritja* moiety myths which are different from the myths of the complementary *Duwa moiety* in that they are about ancestral spirits who came from the land rather than the sea. In fact the moieties reflect the division of the Arnhem Land people, the Yolngu, into land and sea people.

Barama emerged from a waterhole at a place called Guludji near the Koolatong with tresses of freshwater weeds clinging to his arms, carrying special wooden sacred emblems called *rangga* (similar to *tjuringa*) which are made from the trunks of saplings and then are decorated. The weeds were not really weeds, but special ceremonial armbands with long feather pendants attached to them. His whole body was covered with watermarks, forming all the patterns and designs which he eventually passed on to the various Yiritja moiety groups, or clans. Barama brought to the Yiritja moiety their sacred objects and designs.

The other cultural hero, Laindjung, emerged at a place called Dhalungu about the same time as Barama. His body was covered with watermarks but he carried no sacred objects. He walked to Gangan where he met Barama and they called the ceremonial leaders of the Yiritja together to perform and then reform their ceremonies.

Barama and Laindjung were similar to missionaries preaching a new religious belief and passing on or changing ceremonies and giving out sacred objects and designs. Barama stayed in one place and left most of the work to Laindjung. He ordered that the sacred objects should be kept from the sight of women and children. Laindjung did not worry about this and openly displayed them and sang the sacred songs in everyone's hearing. Then the *elders* decided to get rid of the heretic. Near Tribal Bay, they ambushed him, climbing trees and casting *spears* down. Laindjung kept on singing. He sank into a swamp, then re-emerged and walked towards Blue Mud Bay where he turned himself into a paperbark tree, called *dhulwu*.

See also *North-eastern Arnhem Land*.

Bardon, Geoff See *Papunya*.

Bark paintings Putting designs on bark is but a way of passing them on to the next generation. The same designs are used in body painting, on *hollow log coffins* and in ground sculptures. The designs often have their origin in the sacred and come directly from the cultural heroes. All Aboriginal art that is termed 'traditional' is spiritual in that as the artist works he or she is conscious of the spiritual presence and power of the ancestral being whose story is being told or incidents from whose life are being depicted.

The abstract cross-hatched designs which are natural features of many bark paintings are symbolic of a certain area or feature which came from the Great Ancestors themselves. For example *Luma Luma the giant*, who figures prominently in the Mardayan ceremonies at Oenpelli in *Arnhem Land*, cut criss-cross patterns into his flesh, and these are used today in ceremony and also as designs on the bark paintings from this area.

Until recently, the artists used natural *red* and *yellow ochres*, white kaolin or pipeclay and *black* manganese or charcoal. These colours are applied to sheets of bark which have been cured and straightened over a *fire*.

Bark painting was once practised by many *Aboriginal* groups, but since the invasion the tradition has lapsed in most parts of Australia. Today the most vibrant expression is in Arnhem Land. There are different styles of painting here. The artists of west Arnhem Land, which is centred around Oenpelli, the Liverpool and Alligator rivers and the Croker and Goulburn islands, create works which are related to the *rock paintings* which abound in the area, some fine examples of which may be seen in the cave galleries found in *Kakadu National Park*. There are two main types of painting, both of which are figurative. One is the so-called 'X-ray style', in which the ritually significant internal organs of various animal species are depicted. The second style is of spirits such as the stick-like *mimi spirits*.

Central Arnhem Land stretches from east of the Liverpool river and includes the settlements of Maningrida, Ramingining and the island of Milingimbi. Here the paintings are divided into a number of panels, much in the style of a storyboard or comic strip. The most common themes are episodes from the song cycles of the *Wawilak sisters* and Dhanggawul. *North-eastern Arnhem Land* includes the area around Yirrkala and a number of islands, including Galiwinku (Elcho Island), and their styles are characterized by tight geometric compositions and crosshatched patterns of great intricacy.

The *Tiwi people* live on Bathurst and *Melville Islands* off the northwest coast of *Darwin* and most Tiwi art is concerned with the *Pukamani funeral ceremonies*, the elaborate and lengthy ceremonies which involve the erection of carved posts similar to totem poles (see *Pukamani burial poles*). Paintings are usually non-figurative, but sculpture is important here owing to the use of sculpture in the funeral ceremonies. The sculptures are usually of Purukupali, his partner Bima and *Tokumbimi* the bird, and the accompanying myth relates how *death* came to the Tiwi. See *Curlews; Mundungkala; Pukamani funeral ceremonies*.

See also *Bark huts and shelters; Ground paintings; Papunya Tula art*.

Bark huts and shelters Bark huts and shelters were perhaps the most easily erected dwellings of *Aboriginal* people. Depending on the environment, dwellings could be either simple constructions of sheets of bark propped up on a framework; substantial stone houses, as in chilly Victoria; sturdy *miyas* (or *miyu miyas*), sturdy dwellings constructed of boughs and leaves in an igloo shape, as in Western Australia; or a bark or palm frond hut built on a raised platform to escape the *floods* of the rainy season in tropical Australia.

There is a *Dreamtime* story from the *Wik Munggan* people about the Bush-nut husband and wife who constructed one of the first, if not the first hut when the rainy season caught them in the open. Mai Maityi (Bush-nut) husband and wife travelled upriver, hunting and gathering as they went along. The stormy season came on them and they quickly began to cut off sheets of tea-tree bark and lay them on the ground. After this, they cut stakes and placed them in the ground in a circle and tied their tops together. After this, they tied them all around and covered the framework with the sheets of bark. They lit a *fire* inside and took in their food. The rains came, but they were dry and snug inside.

Barra See *Monsoon*.

Barrier Reef The Barrier Reef, lying off the northern coast of Queensland, is one of the wonders of the world. The *Aboriginal* people who live along the coast have passed down stories about when the line of the Barrier Reef was the shore line and when the waters arose.

In the past a man, Gunya, and his two wives were travelling by canoe. They stopped to fish and caught a fish which was taboo. This resulted in a tidal wave arising and rushing towards them. Gunya had a magic *woomera* or spear thrower, an instrument which gives the spear added impetus, called Balur and this warned them of the danger. Gunya placed the magic woomera upright in the prow of his canoe and it calmed the seas enough for them to reach the shore. They hurried towards the mountains and the seas followed them. They reached the top of a mountain and Gunya asked his wives to build a *fire* and heat some large boulders. They rolled the hot stones down at the advancing sea. It stopped there, but never returned to its original home.

Barrukill See *Hydra*.

Bar-wool See *Yarra river and Port Phillip*.

Baskets and bags *Aborigines'* baskets are important containers. Although they are often called *dilly bags*, they are more like baskets than bags, in that they are semi-rigid, unlike the string bags which are also made. Small baskets are used by men to carry sacred objects and in *Aboriginal* mythology they are used for such things as the storing of winds or water. Bags were also made from kangaroo skins and were used for storing water. In some stories it is the piercing of a skin bag which results in *floods*.

There is a central Australia myth about two brothers, one who was prudent and made provision for the future by making a kangaroo skin bag and filling it with water, and the other who did not. The prudent brother refused to share his water with the other when a drought came. He left his bag and went off to hunt. The other brother, maddened by thirst, seized the bag greedily and spilt the water. It gushed out across the sand. The prudent brother saw what was happening and rushed back to save what water he could, but he was too late. The water continued gushing out and filled the hollows and a depression which became part of the sea. Both brothers were drowned in the flood. The birds became alarmed at the spreading flood and attempted to build a dam. They used the roots of a kurrajong tree and this tree became known as the 'water tree'. In times of drought, its roots hold water longer than other trees and can be used as an emergency water supply.

See also *Pukamani funeral ceremonies*.

Bathurst Island See *Tiwi people*.

Beehive The Beehive constellation was Coomartoorung, the smoke of the *fire* of Yuree and Wanjel (Castor and Pollux), two hunters who pursued, caught and then cooked Purra the kangaroo (the star Capella). When the Beehive disappeared from the sky, autumn had begun.

See also *Two Brothers*.

Bellin-Bellin Bellin-Bellin the *crow* is a moiety deity, or ancestor, the opposite to *Bunjil* the eaglehawk. There are many stories of their rivalry. Eaglehawk is a much more sober bird and Crow is renowned for his cunning—though one must be aware from which side the information is coming. A person belonging to the Eaglehawk moiety would tell stories in which Crow would be seen in a bad light and vice versa.

See also *Bunjil; Crow; Eaglehawk and Crow*.

Bennell, Eddie (?—1992) The late Eddie Bennell was a *Nyungar* story-teller from Brookton in the south west who left only a few stories behind. His legacy was seen in Perth when his opera *My Personal Dreaming* was staged in 1993.

Bennett's Brook Bennett's Brook is a stream near Perth, Western Australia, which is sacred to the *Wagyal* or *rainbow snake*. It is an important sacred place to many *Nyungar* people.

See also *Bropho, Robert*.

Berak, William William Berak was an elder of the *Koori* people of Victoria. He lived in the latter part of the nineteenth century.

Through his efforts many of the traditions of the Koori people were passed down. The grave of this great elder is at Healesville, near *Melbourne*.

Berrwah See *Grasshouse mountains*.

Bhima See *Bima*.

Biame (or Baiame, Byamee) Biame the All-Father is perhaps the most important deity of the present-day *Aboriginal* communities in the south-eastern region of Australia and the present mythology has taken into it elements of Christianity.

In the versions of the myth which are told today, Biame is a true creator-god. He experimented first in creating the animals, then used them as models in attempts to create humankind. In the *Dreamtime*, animals were self-conscious and thus had all the discontents of humankind. Kangaroos became ashamed of their tails; fish felt they were imprisoned in water; birds wanted to be like the kangaroos and insects to be larger than they were. Eventually, Biame gathered all the animals together in a cave, took out all their desires and placed them in his new creature: a human being. Thus the animals lost their longings and desires. Men and women alone found themselves the discontented guardians of creation, under the care of the All-Father, who lives up in the *sky world* and gazes down upon his creation. The *Southern Cross* is the visible sign that he watches over humankind and protects us as well as punishing us when we break his laws. Biame created the laws by which humankind are meant to live; he also created the first *bull-roarer* (which when swung represents his voice) and gave the man-making ceremonies to the Aboriginal communities of south-eastern Australia. His chief wife was the All-Mother Birrahgnooloo.

See also *All-Fathers; Boro circles; Crow; Curlews; Ground carvings and sculptures; Kuringgai Chase National Park; Marmoo; Narroondarie; Rainbow snake; Rock engravings; Sleeping giant; Southern Cross; Uniapon, David; Yhi*.

Bibbulmum My people, the Bibbulmum, occupy a corner of south-western Australia and were once made up of a number of groups having different dialects of a single language and similar laws and customs. When the British invaded and settled Western Australia, the tribal basis of our communities was destroyed, especially with the massacre at Pinjarra when the resistance of the people was shattered (see *Yagan*). We have now coalesced into a single people made up of a number of extended families based on the old *tribes*. We now call ourselves *Nyungar*, which simply means 'the people'.

See also *Conception beliefs; Crow; Dogs; Dreaming tracks; Hair string; Seasons; Trade; Willy wagtail; Yagan; Yamadji*.

Bidjigal See *Eora tribe*.

Bildiwuwiju Djanggawul's elder sister. See *Djanggawul and his two sisters myth*.

Bildiwuraru See *Djanggawul and his two sisters myth*.

Bilyarra See *Mars*.

Bima See *Curlews; Mundungkala*.

Bimba-towera the finch See *Echidna*.

Binbeal See *Bunjil*.

Bindirri, Yirri (Roger Solomon) Yirri Bindirri is the son of Malbaru, or James Solomon, and they are both *elders* of the Ngarluma people of Western Australia. They are well known for striving to keep alive the traditions of their people. In the film *Exile and the Kingdom*, the elders explain the mythology which binds them to their country around Roebourne in Western Australia.

Bingingerra the giant freshwater turtle See *Yugumbir people*.

Birbai See *Bundjalung nation*.

Birraarks See *Shamans*.

Birrahgnooloo See *All-Mothers*.

Birrung See *Bundjalung nation*.

Black (or charcoal) is an important colour in *Aboriginal* paintings and also is used as a medicine. It is a sacred colour of the *Yiritja* moiety of *Arnhem Land*.

See also *Bark paintings; Red, black, yellow and white.*

Black flying foxes See *Flying foxes.*

Black Swans See *Altair; Bunjil; Murray river.*

Blood Bird See *Yugumbir people.*

Bloodwood tree See *Djamar; First man child; Menstrual blood; Moiya and pakapaka; Tnatantja poles; Yagan.*

Blue Crane See *Narroondarie.*

Bodngo See *Thunder Man.*

Bolung Bolung is another name for the *rainbow snake* among the people of the Northern Territory. Bolung takes the form of the *lightning* bolt which heralds the approach of the monsoon rains. He is a creative and live-giving deity and, like many of these serpent deities, inhabits deep pools of water.

Bone pointing The bone pointing ceremony in variations is found all over the continent. It is used to kill a person from a distance. The bone is usually made from the femur of a kangaroo or a human, the most powerful pointer being one from the leg of a former shaman.

The ceremony must be performed by a shaman, usually assisted by a colleague. The bone is pointed in the direction of the intended victim. It is said that a *quartz crystal* passes from the point and through space into the victim. The connection is made and the soul of the victim is caught and drawn into the bone through the power of the shaman. Then a lump of wax or clay is quickly attached to the point. This lump, energized by a spell, is to stop the soul escaping from the point. When the soul is caught, the bone is buried in *emu* feathers and native tobacco leaves. It is left in the earth for several months. At the end of this period it is dug up and burnt. As the bone burns, the victim burns along with it, becoming progressively sicker. When the bone is completely consumed, he is dead.

Boomerang The boomerang is more than a bent throwing stick that returns. It was first fashioned from the *tree between heaven and earth*; it symbolizes the rainbow and thus the *rainbow snake*; and the bend is the connection between the opposites, between heaven and *earth*, between *Dreamtime* and ceremony, the past and the present.

In many communities the boomerang is a musical instrument rather than a weapon. Two boomerangs clapped together provide the rhythmic accompaniment in ceremonies, thus creating the connection between *dance* and song.

See also *Gulibunjay and his magic boomerang*.

Boonah See *Narroondarie*.

Bootes The Bootes constellation, or, rather, a star in Bootes, west of *Arcturus*, was Weet-kurrk, daughter of Marpean-kurrk (Arcturus) according to the *Koori*s of Victoria.

Bornumbirr See *Morning Star*.

Boro circles The boro circles or grounds are the sacred ceremonial grounds of the Australian *Aborigine*s. In the eastern regions they consist of a larger and smaller circular ground connected by a path. The smaller boro ground is said to represent the *Sky-World* where *Biame* has his home. It is forbidden to non-initiates. The larger ground represents the *earth* and is public. The ceremonies performed there are less secret.

Boro circles occur all over Australia and have different names in the different *languages*. In regard to these circles, *Bill Neidjie* says, 'This "outside" story. Anyone can listen, Kid, no matter who, but that "inside" story you can't say. If you go in a ring-place, middle of a ring-place, you not supposed to tell im anybody...but, oh, e's nice.'

Borogegal See *Eora tribe*.

Borun the pelican See *Frog*.

Bralgu Bralgu is the *Island of the Dead* according to the *Aboriginal* people of *Arnhem Land*. It is said that after three days the newly deceased is rowed in a canoe by Nganug, an Aboriginal Charon, across the ocean to the Island of the Dead to be greeted by other departed souls.

It is said that every day, shortly before sunset, the souls at Bralgu hold a ceremony in preparation for sending the *Morning Star* to Arnhem Land. During the day and the greater part of the night, the Morning Star is kept in a dilly bag and guarded by a spirit woman called Malumba. The souls and spirits hold a ceremony during which much dust is kicked up. This brings the twilight and then the night to Arnhem Land. When the time approaches for the Morning Star to begin its journey, Malumba releases it from her bag. On release, the Morning Star rises up and rests on a tall pandanus palm tree, the *Dreaming tree of life* and *death*. From there, it looks over the way it is to go, then rises, hovers over the island and ascends high into the sky. Malumba holds a string to which the star is attached, so that it will not run away. When morning comes, Malumba pulls it back and puts it in her bag.

See also *Thunder Man*.

Bram-Bram-Bult See *Centaurus; Southern Cross; Two Brothers*.

Bran Nue Dae *Bran Nue Dae* is a musical put together by Jimmy Chi and the Kuckles Band of Broome. It details the adventures and misadventures of Willie, a young man, and his mentor, Uncle Tadpole, and gives an insight into the modern lifestyles of *Aboriginal* people in Western Australia. It has been enormously successful throughout Australia.

Brisbane See *Dundalli; Grasshouse mountains; Platypus; Rainbow snake*.

Brolga See *Duwa moiety*.

Bropho, Robert Robert Bropho is an important member of the *Nyungar* people who has led the fight to protect the sacred places in Western Australia. He lives in Lockridge on the outskirts of Perth, close to *Bennett's Brook*, an important *Dreaming* place of the Nyungar. He has made films and written books to highlight the injustices of our people and to protect our sacred places.

Buda-buda See *Mopaditis*.

Bull-roarer A bull-roarer is a shaped and incised oval of wood, to one end of which is fastened a string. It is rapidly swung in the boro ground ceremonies (see *Boro circles*). There are many varieties of bull-roarer and the sacredness of the object varies from area to area. When it is incised with sacred designs it becomes a sacred object known as a *tjuringa* or *inma*. In some places it may be seen by everyone; in others, especially in the south east, it may only be seen by the *elders* or initiated men. In some areas, northern Queensland for example, a larger bull-roarer is considered male and a smaller one female. When swung, they are said to be the voices of male and female ancestors, who preside over the sacred ceremonies of initiation. The bull-roarer among the *Kooris* of south-eastern Australia was first made by *Biame* and when it is swung it is said to be his voice.
    See also *Duwoon; Moiya and pakapaka*.

Bullum-Boukan See *Trickster character*.

Bullum-tut See *Trickster character*.

Bumerali See *Universe*.

Bundjalung nation The Bundjalung people are a large *Aboriginal* nation, a federation of a number of groups of clans which occupy the land from the Clarence river of northern New South Wales north to the town of Ipswich in southern Queensland. The names of these groups are Aragwal, Banbai, Birbai, Galiabal, Gidabal, Gumbainggeri, Jigara, Jugambal, Jugumbir, Jungai, Minjungbal, Ngacu, Ngamba, Thungutti and Widjabal. Their ancestors are the three brothers, Mamoon, Yar Birrain and Birrung, who are said to have come from the sea. The brothers, along with their grandmother, arrived in a canoe made from the bark of a hoop pine. As they followed the coastline, they found a rich land sparsely populated. They landed at the mouth of the Clarence river and stayed there for a long time, then, leaving their grandmother behind, they continued on in their canoe heading up the east coast. At one place they landed and created a spring of fresh water. They stopped along the coast at various places and populated the land. They made the laws for the Bundjalung and also the ceremonies of the *boro circle*.
    It is said that the blue haze over the distant mountains,

especially in spring, is the daughters of the three brothers revisiting the Earth to ensure its well-being and continuing fertility.

See also *Bundjalung National Park; Dogs; Duwoon; Ginibi, Ruby Langford; Gold Coast; Great battles; Jalgumbun; Terrania Creek basin and cave; Tooloom Falls; Woollool Woollool*.

Bundjalung National Park Bundjalung National Park in northern New South Wales includes Dirrawonga, a sacred goanna site now called Goanna Headland.

In the *Dreamtime*, Nyimbunji, an elder of the *Bundjalung nation*, asked a goanna to stop a snake tormenting a bird. The goanna chased the snake to Evan's Head on the coast where a fight ensued. The goanna took up the chase again and went into the sea. It came out from the sea and became Goanna Headland.

The goanna is associated with rain and there is a rain cave on the headland where the *elders* of the Bundjalung people went in the old days to conduct ceremonies for rain.

See also *Bundjalung nation; Rain-making*.

Bungle Bungles The Bungle Bungles in Western Australia is a taboo area. It covers an area of 700 square kilometres with sheer cliffs, striated walls and deep gullies. The formations were considered to be inhabited by forces inimical to life and so no *Aborigines* ever went there.

Bunitj See *Kakadu National Park; Neidjie, Bill; Seasons*.

Bunjil Bunjil the Eaglehawk ancestor is a creator ancestor of immense power and prestige to the *Kooris*, the modern *Aboriginal* peoples inhabiting what is now the state of Victoria. In the old days he was a moiety deity, or ancestor, of one half of the Kulin people of central Victoria.

Bunjil had two wives and a son, Binbeal, the rainbow, whose wife was the second bow of the rainbow. He is said to be assisted by six *wirnums* or *shamans*, who represent the clans of the Eaglehawk moiety. These are Djurt-djurt the nankeen kestrel, Thara the quail hawk, Yukope the parakeet, Dantum the parrot, Tadjeri the brushtail possum and Turnong the glider possum.

After Bunjil had made the mountains and rivers, the flora and fauna, and given humankind the laws to live by, he gathered his wives and sons, then asked his moiety opposite, *Bellin-Bellin* the *crow*, who had charge of the winds, to open his bags and let out some wind. Bellin-Bellin opened a bag in which he kept his whirlwinds and the resulting cyclone blew great trees into the air, roots and all. Bunjil called for a stronger wind and Bellin-Bellin obliged. Bunjil and his people were whirred aloft to the *sky world* where he became the star *Altair* and his two wives, the *black* swans, the stars on either side.

See also *Eaglehawk and Crow; Melbourne*.

Bunjil Narran See *Shamans*.

Bunuba people The Bunuba people live in the *Kimberley* region of Western Australia and their country is below that of the Worora, Wunambul and *Ngarinjin* peoples. Their main ancestors are Murlu the kangaroo and the Maletji *dogs*, who gave them their laws and customs as well as their land, culture, weapons, songs and ceremonies.

During the resistance led by *Jandamara* against the invaders in the late nineteenth century, the Bunuba people suffered terribly with men, women and children being massacred wherever they were.

See also *Dogs; Woonamurra, Banjo*.

Bunurong people See *Melbourne; Yarra river and Port Phillip*.

Bunya the possum See *Centaurus; Southern Cross*.

Bunyip The Bunyip, a legendary monster, supposedly of *Aboriginal* origin, appears to be an instance of mistaken identity. It seems to be the Meendie giant snake of Victoria who lived in the waterhole near Bunkara-bunnal, or Puckapunya. The attributes of the Bunyip are those of the *rainbow snake*.

Buramedigal See *Eora tribe*.

Burnum Burnum (1936–) is an elder of the Wurandjeri people of southern New South Wales. He is a story-teller, actor and worker for his people. In 1988 he went to England to claim that country on behalf of all *Aboriginal* people as compensation for the wrongs inflicted on our people by the invaders from that island. He has become well-known for popularizing a dolphin *Dreaming* ceremony.

Burrajahnee See *Dogs*.

Burrajan See *Dogs*.

Burrawungal See *Water sprites*.

Burriway the emu See *Great corroborees*.

Burrup peninsula Burrup peninsula in the Pilbara was owned by the Yaburara people. In the nineteenth century they were completely wiped out in what is called the Flying Foam Massacre. Their land is now cared for by the *Ngarluma people*.

The peninsula is a natural gallery of figures pecked into the hard rock. There are over 4,000 motifs in the area. One of the most interesting sites shows figures climbing (perhaps away from a flood?) *Parraruru* (Robert Churnside), now deceased, relates a flood story of this region. Pulpul, Cuckoo, was then a man and lived on the peninsula. The sea began rising. He thought what to do about it. It rose and rose, then he said 'Down, down.' It went down and he became a bird just at that moment.

In another story from the neighbouring Jindjiparndi people, the seas rose until they flooded the land 30 miles inland before being stopped by Pulpul. It is said that mangroves still grow there.

Bush-nut husband and wife See *Bark huts and shelters*.

Byamee See *Biame*.

Byron Bay Byron Bay in northern New South Wales is close to an important woman's fertility site situated at Broken Head.

Lorraine Mafi-Williams, an important woman story-teller and custodian of culture, lives in the town.

C

The canoe maker

Canis Major The Wotjobaluk *Koori* people of Victoria believed that the small star between the larger ones on the body of Canis Major was Unurgunite and the two larger ones were his wives. The one furthermost away was the wife *Mityan the moon* fell in love with.

Canoes Canoes are said to have come from the ancestors of the *Dreamtime*, as with all weapons and artefacts.

The first bark canoe was invented by Goanna the monitor lizard, who is associated with the bark of trees because he is always running up and down them. It is said that once in the Dreamtime Goanna was a man and decided to make a canoe. He stripped off a large sheet of bark from a tree and sewed it up, then got in and went off to spear fish, but the canoe was no good and badly leaked. He left it behind and went upriver until he found a mess-mate tree. He again cut out a large sheet of bark. He placed it across a *fire* to dry it out and to make it pliable, then cut fine bamboo, burnt the point in fire, split the stalk down, flattened it and cut it into strips with his knife. He folded the sheet of bark down the middle and sewed one end pushing the point of the cane through holes pierced by a wallaby-bone awl. He sewed up the other end. Then he cut off the short ends slantwise, inwards and downwards. He cut some short sticks, put a stick on each side, laying them crosswise to keep the canoe stretched outwards, then fastened the bark to the sticks by strong string. He cut the splayed foot of a magrove stem into a paddle, planed it down, heated it over the fire and straightened it. Thus the second and better canoe was made.

See also *Murray river; Seagull and Torres Strait Pigeon; Thunder Man.*

Canopus The star Canopus, according to some groups of *Koori* people, was the *moeity ancestor* Waa (*Crow*).

See also *Rober Carol; Sirius; Taboo countries; Tasmanian creation myth.*

Cape York peninsula Cape York peninsula in the far north of Queensland is the home of different groups of people such as the Gugu-Yalanji, Gugu-Imudji, Gugu-Almura, Gugu-Warra and others.

In this area are the rock galleries at *Laura* which give pictorial detail of the desperate resistance waged by the people there against the invaders and their *Aboriginal* allies.

See also *Crocodiles; Dilly bags; Dogs; Giant dogs; Goolbalathaldin; Great corroborees; Matchwood tree; Mbu the ghost; Peewit, the protector of husbands; Quinkin; Sorcery figures; Taipan; Wik Munggan; Yams.*

Capella See *Beehive.*

Capricornus The double star in the head of the Capricornus constellation represented the fingers of Collenbitjik the bull-ant, when he was rescuing the body of his nephew, Totyerguil (*Altair*) from the deep pool inhabited by a giant water snake.

Castor and Pollux See *Two Brothers.*

Centaurus The constellation of Centaurus had various mythological symbolism attached to it by different *Koori* groups.

The two stars in the forelegs of Centaurus were the *Two Brothers,* the Bram-Bram-Bult. They speared and killed Tjingal the *emu*, who is represented by the dark space between the forelegs of Centaurus and the *Southern Cross*. Tjingal was pursuing Bunya the possum, represented by the star at the head of the Southern Cross, when he was speared by the Bram-Bram-Bult.

The Kulin *community* of Kooris believed that the two stars in Centaurus were two of *Bunjil's* shamans, Djurt-djurt and Thara, possibly the names of two clans of the Eaglehawk moiety.

See also *Inma boards*.

Charcoal See *Black*.

Cherbourg Aboriginal settlement Cherbourg *Aboriginal* settlement in Queensland is on the borders of the countries of the Waka Waki and Kabi peoples. It is the place where the Murri poet and story-teller Lionel Fogarty was born. On Barambah Creek, a little upstream of the settlement, is a large rock which juts out into the stream. Lionel tells a story about how a strange man who was looking for his home appeared on the rock one night and called out: 'Booyu-u-u, booyu-u-u, booyubill, booyubill, booyubill-bill-bill.' The Waka Waka and Kabi people thought he was laughing at them and attacked him with *spears*. Two spears struck him, then a shaman called out: 'Sue, be a bird, Booyooburra, and then laugh at us from that rock.' The booyooburra man changed into a stone plover, then into a curlew with long legs like spears.

Chi, Jimmy See *Bran Nue Dae*.

Childbirth Childbirth in the old days was strictly women's business and the subject was taboo to men. During childbirth a woman lived apart from the main camp with a few womenfolk. No man could approach her camp or speak to her.

In this women's myth from the *Wik Munggan* people, the birthing procedure as laid down in the *Dreamtime* by the *black* snake man and his wife the dove is described.

Yuwam the black snake and Kolet the dove were once husband and wife and lived by a river, travelling up and down its banks. The wife is heavy with child and when her time comes upon her, she sits down while her husband goes away. She kneels, sitting on her knees as the contractions begin. The head appears and she guides the baby out and onto the ground. She holds the cord and begins calling out names. She calls names one after the other until the cord gives way and then she knows that she has found the baby's proper name. She repeats this name as the afterbirth comes out. All is over and she lays the baby on a sheet of paperbark.

The man comes back and sits a short distance from her. 'I wonder what it is,' he says, as if to himself. 'It's a man child,' she says, as if to herself. She sits by herself, then lies down. The baby cries and she gives him her breast.

For five days the mother lies resting. Her husband brings her *yams*, always the same, but neither of them eat any fish, lest the baby grow sick and die. The husband cooks the yams and lays them a little way off from his wife. After five days, she says aloud to herself, 'It is finished.' The man goes fishing, catches some fish. He lights the *fire*, breaks the neck of the fish and cooks them. He eats a small catfish and a knight-fish, then lays some aside for the evening meal. The woman now goes to look for her own yams. As the fluid is still flowing, she is not allowed to eat fish. She is not allowed to eat any of the fish her husband catches, nor can he eat any of the yams she digs up.

After about six days, when the woman's flow stops, she can take the baby to her husband. She puts the yams and some small fish she has caught into three *dilly bags*, filling them right to the top. One bag is for herself, one is for her husband and the third is for the baby. She has made a string apron and puts this on. She smears her face with clay and her body with ashes, putting white clay on her forehead. She rubs charcoal over the baby's body and a white smear of paint on his nose. She breaks off the navel cord to give to her husband. She fastens a beeswax pendant to it, striped with strips of yellow bark, and then ties the cord around the neck of the baby. Picking up the dilly bags, she hangs one from her head, slings another across her shoulder and her chest to hang under the arm, then places the third one on her head. She then goes to the father.

She lies the baby in his arms and after a time he smears it with sweat, rubbing it over the forehead and face. He then takes the cord and places it around his own neck. The mother places the yams beside her husband, then picks up a dilly bag and rubs it across the mouth of the baby, so that he will not always be crying. Finally, she lies on her stomach, saying, 'So that he will not always be running after others for food, but will come running back to us, and we will always keep together.'

After this, in this Dreamtime story, the woman, the dove, Kolet, returned to her own *djang* or *auwa* place and the black snake man and his son returned to his.

See also *Conception beliefs; First man child; Spirit children*.

Churinga See *Tjuringa*.

Churnside, Robert See *Parraruru*.

Collenbitjik See *Altair; Capricornus; Murray river*.

Coma Berenices The star group Coma Berenices was seen by the *Koori* people of Victoria as a flock of small birds drinking water which filled the hollow in the fork of a tree.

Community 'Community', as distinct from 'tribe', means the local ties which began when *Aboriginal* people were concentrated together by the Europeans at certain localities or on reserves and missions without attention being paid to tribal differences. They were often made up of peoples speaking different *languages* and over time one language came to predominate, whether a variety of English or an Aboriginal language, for instance Walmatjarri in the *Kimberley* region of Western Australia around Fitzroy Crossing. It is from such concentrations that regional names for *Aborigines* developed, such as *Koori*, Goori or Boori in Victoria and New South Wales, Murri in Queensland, *Nanga* in parts of South Australia, Nungar or *Nyungar* in south-western Australia and Yolngu in *Arnhem Land*.

See also *Kin groups; Trade; Tribes*.

Conception beliefs Many *Aborigines*, including my people, the *Bibbulmum*, believed that *spirit children* inhabited certain fertility sites. They were either left there by the ancestors in the *Dreamtime* or were souls awaiting reincarnation. They waited there for a suitable opportunity to enter a womb. Women who wished to have a child went to these places. It was believed that although a male had some part in conception, he more or less opened up the passage for the spirit child to enter. The most important aspect, if a woman was to become pregnant, was the presence and entry of a spirit child.

See also *Childbirth; First man child; Menstrual blood; Spirit children*.

Coolamon The coolamon is an all-purpose wooden carrying dish found all across Australia. Some are intricately carved.

Coomartoorung See *Beehive*.

Coonowrin See *Grasshouse mountains*.

Cooper, William (?–1941) William Cooper was a *Koori* elder who led a tribal revitalization movement in the 1930s. He created an 'Aboriginal Day of Mourning' in 1938 and an 'Aboriginal Sunday' annual Koori day. He led the fight in those days for equal rights and justice for all *Aborigines*.

Corkwood sisters See *Katatjuta*.

Corona Borealis Corona Borealis was the *boomerang* thrown by Totyerguil (*Altair*) at the giant snake before it dragged him down into the depths of a deep pool and drowned him.

Corroboree Corroboree is a *Koori* word, perhaps from the Eora language, which has been taken into English. Roughly, it means a *dance* or ceremony. The suffix 'boree' shows that it refers to the *boro circles*, or ceremonial grounds.

Cosmography The cosmography of the *Aboriginal* people of Australia was roughly similar all across the continent. The *Earth* was a flat circular body covered with a concave sky which reached down to the horizon. The sky was the earth of another plane or world which was a rich country with a plentiful water supply. Many *ancestral beings* and cultural heroes lived there. The stars are said to be either these beings or their campfires. Underneath our world was an *underworld*, similar to ours and inhabited by people much like ourselves.

Among the *Kooris* it was believed that the sky was raised on props placed at the extreme corners of the Earth. An old man who lived on the high plains was in charge of the eastern prop. During and just after the British invasion news came south that the eastern prop was rotting and if tools were not sent to the old man, he could not repair it and the sky would fall, killing everyone. It is said that the news filled everyone with consternation and many stone axes were sent north.

See also *Galaxy; Moon; Sky world; Stars and constellations; Sun;*

Universe.

Creation myths Creation myths are those stories which tell us how the landscape came into being and how animals and plants received their shapes and markings and the importance of these markings. Encoded within the shapes and markings of animals are the traces which go towards sanctioning the laws and customs of particular tribal groups.

For example, one story of the Native Cat and the *Black*-headed Python, told by the Worora people in north-western Australia, provides the sanction for the rule that a widow covers herself with ashes during her period of mourning. In the *Dreamtime*, the Native Cat and his wife, the Black-headed Python, lived alone. The Native Cat became sick and got sores all over his body. The spots the Native Cat has today are where these sores were. Black-headed Python tried to cure him, but eventually he died. She buried him, then went on eastward, alone. She came to a place where a goanna was buried and poked at it. She called the place Marngut, then continued on until she came to a smaller hill, Wunjaragin, or Loose Mountain, as it seemed to be falling apart. She gathered it up in her hand and tried to tie it together with her hair, but it kept on crumbling. Finally, some bull ants came along and helped her to keep it together. Then she went on further.

In the meantime the Blue-tongued Lizard, who had heard her crying when her husband had died, came to his grave and resurrected him. Together they went on to search for Black-headed Python. At last they came up to her, but when the Python saw her husband, she cried out, 'No, go back to your grave. I'm a widow now. I have cut off all my hair and am bald. I have rubbed charcoal over my face so that people will know that I am a widow. Go back to your grave, re-enter it and die.'

Native Cat did so. Ever since this time, widows have followed the Python's example and cut off their hair and rubbed their faces with charcoal to show their sorrow at the loss of their husbands. As was done in the *Dreaming* or Dreamtime, so shall be done today.

In translating creation myths into English and in changing the stories, Europeans have obscured the wisdom passed down by the Australian *Aborigines* from generation to generation. The creation myth or story is but one aspect of the whole and must be linked with the sacred place, sacred song and sacred ceremony known only to the fully initiated *elders* of each tribe.

See also *All-Fathers; All-Mothers; Ancestral beings; Biame; Dreamtime; Eaglehawk and Crow; First woman; Flinders Range; Glasshouse mountains; Melville Island; Mundungkala; Tasmanian creation myth; Walbiri creation myth; Women ancestral beings.*

Creation Time, the See *Dreamtime*.

Crocodiles There are two types of crocodile in Australia: the freshwater crocodile (*Crocodilus johnstoni*) and the saltwater crocodile (*Crocodilus porosus*). The freshwater crocodile inhabits *waterholes* and freshwater streams in northern Australia and is relatively harmless. The saltwater crocodile is man-eating, dangerous and greatly feared. It inhabits the saltwater estuaries, going out and coming in with the tide after fish.

Among the *Wik Munggan* people of the *Cape York peninsula* and other peoples of northern Australia, Pikuwa, the saltwater crocodile, is considered wily, sly and a great coward. Not only this, he is also feared as a wife-stealer and a rapist.

A Wik Munggan myth shows his character. One day two girls were looking for mud-mussels. They were all alone, picking up the mud-shells, placing them in the ashes of a *fire* and eating them. They ate all they had and decided to go and get some more. They crawled on their knees, searching out the mud-mussels with their hands and putting them in their *dilly bags*.

At last they had enough, returned to the fire and cooked them. They decided to keep some for their father and called out for him to bring the canoe. There was a return shout. 'Father, bring the canoe,' they called again, not realizing that it was Pikuwa. Aroused, but having no canoe, he descended into the water, feeling his way along the muddy bottom with his hands. He reached the girls and his nose and back came out from the water. The girls screamed out in alarm.

'Up you get on my back, you two. Come along, jump on my back,' he said.

Attracted in spite of themselves, the girls jumped on his back and he carried them across the stream. On the other side, they jumped off and laughed at him, and he flirted with them. Just then their father and mother came to the opposite bank.

'You two girls, what are you doing?' they called.

'Father and mother, come over here,' they shouted back.

Pikuwa went across the stream, showed his back, told the parents to jump on and brought them across. They began eating the mud-mussels, and Pikuwa sank down in the mud and watched them.

Then the younger sister found *honey* in an iron-wood tree and the father chopped a hole in the trunk and collected it. He took as much as he could in his wooden vessel, then decided to return to their camp. The two girls told their parents to go ahead. They kept poking in the tree with a stick and licking up the honey.

Pikuwa continued watching them. Then he sank down into the mud in the water, made a hole, dug deeper and deeper and made a passage towards the girls. He found the root of the iron-wood tree and went inside it and up into the hollow trunk from where the girls were getting the honey. They poked in their stick to get more and he called out, 'Hey, I'm a man, you shouldn't poke me like that!'

Alarmed, they ran away. Pikuwa left the tree trunk the same way he had entered. He rose up from the water and looked around. He could not see the girls, but he saw the path they had taken and rushed after them. He heard them calling for their father and he answered. They called again and he told them to hurry up and come. The two girls came to where he was waiting and he raped them. Then he carried them off on his back, stopping on the way to rape them again.

Finally, he said that he was going to dig a hole and did so. He came out from it, told the two girls to lie down and raped them again. He went back to his hole to dig again, stopped and came out and raped them again. He went back to his hole again and the girls decided to block up the entrance. They gathered branches and poked them in. They poked in more and more, then rolled a log against the entrance. 'Now, let's run,' they said, and rushed along the track to their mother and father. They told their parents that they had been raped by Pikuwa, not once but many times.

Meanwhile Pikuwa felt aroused again. He crawled toward the entrance and struck the wood blocking it. Undaunted, he made a smaller passage around the obstruction and came out. He went after the girls and came up to them, but the father was hiding behind a tree. He had plenty of *spears* and his spear-thrower too. He threw spear after spear and all of them hit Pikuwa. Finally, he took up his tomahawk and struck Pikuwa on the forehead again and again. With his knife he cut off Pikuwa's head and with their yamsticks the women poked him in the anus, then hacked off his penis and cut it into pieces. Finally, they made a huge fire and cooked him up. 'You can make your *djang* place here,' they said, 'Katyapikanam Auwa [Hit on the Head], for here you, Pikuwa, were hit on the head.'

There are other myths detailing Pikuwa's enormous sexual appetites. In the *Dreamtime*, Kena and Pikuwa were men. Warka, Swamp Turtle, was Kena's wife. Pikuwa and Warka began an illicit love affair and ran off together. Waka, Flying Fox, betrayed their location to Kena. He rushed there and began fighting with Pikuwa. First they wrestled with their hands, then Kena stabbed

Pikuwa in the ribs with a spear thrust. Pikuwa picked up a fire-brand and hit Kena with it on the back of the neck. His neck became swollen. At last Kena lay there weary and exhausted. Pikuwa left him and went westwards to the sea to get well in the salt water. It is there that he makes his home.

See also *Jirakupai; Numuwuwari.*

Crow (Waa; Wahn) Crow holds a very important place in the mythology of the Australian *Aborigines*. To many he is a *moiety ancestor* and those belonging to his moiety are called 'Crow people'. The area of Perth where I live was once the land of the *Bibbulmum*, who belong to this moiety, and the Crow is still held in respect to this day.

Crow often is a *trickster character*, in sharp contrast to his more sombre moiety counterpart, *Bunjil* the eaglehawk. A *Koori* myth from Victoria tells how Crow stole *fire* from the seven women guardians. In the *Dreamtime* only these seven women knew the secret of fire and refused to divulge how it was made. Crow decided that he would get their secret. He made friends with the women and found out that they carried fire at the ends of their digging sticks. He also found out that the women were fond of termites, but afraid of snakes. He buried a number of snakes in a termite mound, then told the women he had found a large nest of termites. They followed him to the spot and broke open the mound. The snakes attacked them and they defended themselves with their digging sticks. This caused fire to fall from the sticks. Quickly, Crow picked up the fire between two pieces of bark and ran away. Now Crow in his turn refused to share fire with anyone. Every time someone asked him, he mockingly called out, 'Waa, waa.' He caused so much strife that even he at last lost his temper and threw coals at some of the men who were pestering him for fire. The coals caused a bushfire in which he supposedly was burnt to *death*, but the eternal trickster came to life and the survivors heard his mocking 'Waa, waa' echoing from a large tree.

The Woiwurong Koori people's *elders* told a similar myth of how once there were seven young women called the Karatgurk who lived on the Yarra river where *Melbourne* now stands. They lived on *yams* which they dug out with their digging sticks, on the end of which they also carried live coals. They kept the fire to themselves. They cooked their own yams, but gave raw ones to Crow. One day Crow found one of the cooked yams and tasted it. He found it delicious and decided to cook his yams from then on. The women refused to give him fire and so he decided to trick them out of it. He caught and hid a lot of snakes in an ant mound, then called to the girls that he had found a large ant mound and that the ant larvae tasted much better than yams. The women ran to the mound and began digging into it with their sticks. The snakes came hissing out and chased them away, screaming. But then the women turned and began to hit out at the snakes with their digging sticks. They hit so hard that some of the live coals were knocked off. Crow was waiting for this. He pounced on the live coals and hid them in a kangaroo skin bag he had prepared. When the women had killed all the snakes, they came back to look for the coals. They could not find them and decided that Crow had taken them. They chased him, but he flew out of reach and perched on the top of a very high tree.

Bunjil saw what had happened and asked Crow for some of the coals, as he wanted to cook a possum. Crow offered to cook it for him and when he had done so, threw it down to Eaglehawk who saw that it was still smoking. He tried to blow it into flame, but failed. He ate the possum and while he did so, the Koori people gathered around and shouted at Crow to give them fire. The din scared him and at last he flung some live coals at the crowd. Kurok-goru the fire-tailed finch picked up some of the coals and hid them behind his back and that is why these finches have red tails. Eaglehawk's shaman helpers, Djurt-djurt the nankeen kestrel and Thara the quail hawk, grabbed the rest of the coals.

Then the coals made a bush fire which burnt Crow *black*. It also spread over his country and Bunjil had to gather all the Kooris to help put it out. He placed some rocks at the head of the Yarra river to stop the fire spreading that way, and they are there to this day. His two helpers were burnt and became two rocks at the foot of the Dandenong Range. The Karatgurk were swept up into the sky where they became the *Pleiades*, the stars representing their glowing firesticks.

Crow is perhaps one of the most attractive and entertaining of the *ancestral beings*. He lived and passed on in mirth. Towards the end of his stay on *Earth*, he was travelling down the *Murray river* when he came across Swamp Hawk. Crow decided to play a trick on the bird. He planted *echidna* quills in the deserted nest of a kangaroo rat and got Swamp Hawk to jump on them. One of the interesting things about many of Crow's tricks is that they benefit the person he plays them on, and in this case Swamp Hawk was pleased, for the quills grew into his feet and he found that he could catch kangaroo rats easily.

Crow continued on his journey and became caught in a storm. The rain lashed down and he felt cleansed by it. It was then that a voice was heard. It was *Biame* the All-Father. He took the old Crow up into the sky where he became the star *Canopus*.

See also *Balayang; Bellin-Bellin; Bunjil; Eaglehawk and Crow; Rober Carol; Sirius*.

Curlews Among some *Aboriginal tribes* curlews are the guardians of the dear departed. Their evening cry is a warning of *death*: it tells people that the bird is on his way to carry the soul of the dead person to the *sky world*.

Oodgeroo of the Noonuccal people tells the story of how curlews were once men belonging to a tribe which stayed close to the earth and never slept by night. They stayed awake to give warning if danger threatened those they loved. The All-Father *Biame* admired them for this and came to them and offered to reward them. They asked that they be changed into birds and be made guardians of the departed ones. Biami granted them their wish and so now the curlew carries the souls of the departed to the sky world, but first he gives a warning cry on three successive nights, so that the people will not be afraid and will know that the death will be from natural causes.

Curlews' connection to death is also found in the great corpus of myths which govern the *Pukamani funeral ceremonies* of the *Tiwi people* of *Melville Island*. It is told that when the ancestral being Purukupali heard that his son Djinini had died, owing to the misconduct of his wife, Bima, with the *moon*, Japara, he first attacked Japara, then walked into the sea with his dead son in his arms. His death initiated a great change on the world. Japara became the moon and rose into the sky with the wounds made in the battle with Purukupali visible on his face. Bima became a curlew and roams the forest at night wailing with remorse and sorrow at the loss of her son and the calamity she brought to the world.

Cut hair and nail parings Cut hair and nail parings were always collected and burnt as they could be used in magic against the person from whom they came.

Cyclops (or Papinjuwaris) are one-eyed giants who, according to the *Tiwi people* of *Melville Island*, live in a large hut where the sky ends. Shooting stars are said to be a Papinjuwari stalking across the heavens with a blazing firestick in one hand and a fighting club in the other. They are also said to crave the bodies of the dead and the blood of the sick for food. A Papinjuwari locates a sick person by smell and then makes himself invisible and sucks the blood from the arm of the victim without leaving a wound. As the sick person becomes weaker, the Papinjuwari makes himself small enough to enter the body through the mouth and drinks up the rest of the blood.

D

Dilly bag

Dance Dance plays an important part in the lives and cultures of *Aboriginal* people, and even in those areas heavily influenced by British culture, where many of the ceremonies have been lost, no Aboriginal event is complete without traditional dance.

Aboriginal dance is often a pantomimic representation of some major event, spiritual tradition or myth, and dances are linked into series which may go on for several days or nights. These series are dramatic performances, each section ending on a highnote which increases the excitement up to the final dance sequence.

See also *Boomerang; Corroboree; Djanggawul mythology and ceremonies; Great corroborees; Laura; Luma Luma the giant; Palga; Rom ceremony of Arnhem Land; Seagull and Torres Strait Pigeon.*

Dantum the parrot See *Bunjil*.

Daramulun See *All-Fathers*.

Darwin Darwin, the capital of the Northern Territory and gate-way to *Kakadu National Park*, is in the country of the Larrakia people. There are a number of sacred sites within the city's bound-aries, including Gundal-Madlamaning (Emery Point) and Kulaluk. Kulaluk has on it part of the *Aboriginal* settlement of Bagot. Since the mid-1970s the Larrakia people have continued a struggle to protect their sacred *djang* sites from the encroachment of the city.

See also *Palga*.

Davis, Jack (1917–) Jack Davis is a *Nyungar* writer and play-wright who has detailed the culture and history of the *Aboriginal* people of south-western Australia in his plays.

Death There are many accounts of how death came into the world. In many, if not all communities, there is a belief in the con-tinuing existence of an essence or ghost or soul after death, and the necessity of sending it on its way, or back to the *Dreaming* site of its ancestor where it waits to be reborn (see also *Conception beliefs*).

In some communities, the soul is sent along the road to the *Island of the Dead*, from whence it ascends to a *sky world* if it remembers the correct rites to ensure its passage, otherwise it may become lost.

The *moon* is important in beliefs about death. The *elders* of the Kulin *community* in Victoria relate how the moon or moonman used to revive those who died with a drink of the elixir of immor-tality, much like the *amrita* of the Hindus, which is also located on the moon and over which the gods and demons fought long ago. In the Kulin story, Pigeon was jealous of the power of the moon and counteracted the effect of the elixir so that those who died remained dead—as men and women have done ever since. Only the moon escaped death and comes to life every month.

In *Arnhem Land*, the moon is called Alinda. It is related that in the *Dreamtime* he lived with Dirima the parrot fish and they were always quarrelling. During one particularly fierce quarrel they began fighting and wounded each other. Alinda then ascended to the sky as the moon, while Dirima withdrew to the sea as the parrot fish. The marks of the fight can still be seen on Alinda. He cursed the parrot fish and all living things with death. The curse also affected him, but after dying he is reborn again. It is said that the skeleton of the dead moon falls into the ocean where it is found as the chambered nautilus shell.

See also *Bralgu; Curlews; Dhambidj song series of Arnhem Land; Dorabauk; Hollow log coffins; Matchwood tree; Mbu the ghost;*

Mopaditis; Morning Star; Mundungkala; Owl; Pukamani funeral ceremonies; Relics of the dead; Smoking; Taipan.

Delphinus The Delphinus star is seen by the *Koori* people living along the banks of the *Murray river* as Otjout the cod fish, who made the Murray river whilst escaping from Totyerguil (*Altair*).

Depuch Island See *Warmalana*.

Dewaliwall See *Mornington Island*.

Dhagay the sand goanna See *Great corroborees*.

Dhambidj song series of Arnhem Land The Dhambidj songs are usually sung at funerals. They are about the spirit ancestors of the *Aborigines* around the Blyth river in *Arnhem Land*. The verses evoke the ancestors and the ceremonies which lay the dear departed to rest and send them on their way. Songs such as 'Crow, Hollow Log and Sugar Bag' bear directly on the ceremonies and have great symbolic value.

There are 21 songs in the series, and an enumeration of their titles gives a list of the important ancestors of this area. They are: '*Black* Bittern', 'Turtle', '*Marrawal* [Spirit Man]', 'Yam', 'Djurdidjurda Bird', 'Marsupial Mouse', 'Friar Bird', 'Bandicoot', 'Wild Honey and Hollow Log', 'King Brown Snake', 'White Cockatoo', '*Crow*', 'Eel' and others. 'Hollow Log' is particularly evocative of the funeral service and shows how honey is equated with the renewal of all life:

Tree trunk, tree wood; tree trunk, tree wood;
Dry tree, hollow log; hot, dark honey, full to overflowing;
dry wood, filled with honey; dry wood living at
Djubordaridja; tree wood filled with dark wild honey;
Tree wood; honey oozing from the cut cells; hot, dark honey
oozing; dry wood filled with honey; dry tree living at
Djubordaridja;
Inside the tree wild honey ferments;
Tree's dung; wad of straw sucks up the sweet honey; hollow
tree, dry log; coffin named badurra cut from hollow tree;
honey spirit women hang up their baskets at Garinga and
Djubordaridja.

See also *Death; Pukamani funeral ceremonies.*

Dhuwa moiety See *Duwa moiety*.

Didjeridoo (or Yidaka) The didjeridoo is a long wooden tube made from the hollow bough of a tree. It is used by *Aboriginal* people all across Australia. It represents male energy and the playing of it by women is forbidden. In effect it is a deity in and by itself, the phallus of an ancestor, and there are strict instructions encoded in song verses which should be chanted when it is made or played. If it is made and energized in the proper way, when it is called upon, it will almost play itself. It is a powerful instrument of healing in its own right.

See also *Oobarr*.

Dieri See *Diyari people*.

Dilly bags The making of the first dilly bags is credited to an old woman ancestor by the clans of the *Wik Munggan*. Her sacred place in *Cape York peninsula* is called Waiyauwa, 'the place of the old woman'.

Once many women had come to this place to make dilly bags and a mother said to her daughter, 'Let us make a fine dilly bag. Bring fibre from the *ngangka* [fig tree] and we will make a *wangka* [net bag]. Now bring some white fibre from the *tu-ta* [palm leaf].'

The daughter brought the fibre to her mother, enough for them both and she began working on the *wangka* she was making out of the white fibre woven in the weave used in making 'grass' baskets. They made many dilly bags with a wide weave with which they gathered *yams* and squeezed them through the mesh.

When they had finished eating they placed the dilly bags they had made into a canoe and got in. They had made dilly bags from fig tree fibre, dilly bags made from the white fibre from the leaves of a palm tree, dilly bags made from the red fibre of the acacia, and dilly bags made in the fish net stitch. The canoe was overloaded with dilly bags. In the middle of the river, the canoe became caught in the current, spun round and round and started to sink. As it sank, the women sang a song about the old woman who made the first dilly bags.

See also *Baskets and bags; Childbirth*.

Dinderi See Platypus.

Dingoes See *Dogs*.

Dirima the parrot fish See *Death*.

Dirrangan See *Tooloom Falls*.

Dirrawonga See *Bundjalung National Park*.

Diyari people The Diyari (or Dieri) people lived on the eastern shores of Lake Eyre in central Australia. In 1866 German Lutheran missionaries established a mission at Lake Killalpaninna in which most of the Diyari were concentrated, together with other Aborigines of the region who spoke different *languages*. Following the disastrous influenza epidemic of 1919 which decimated the mission population, it closed in 1920. The Diyari are a very spiritual people and encoded their spiritual beliefs in sculptures which are called *Toa*.

See also *Extinct giant marsupials; Jinabuthina; Palkalina; Toa sculptures*.

Djabi See *Parraruru*.

Djamar Djamar mythology relates to the cultural hero Djamar, who established many of the laws, rites and ceremonies of the west *Kimberley* region of Western Australia.

Djamar came from the sea at a place called Bulgin, where he rested for three days against a paperbark tree. The Djamar myth is enacted in ceremonies and songs, and this event is celebrated in a short verse:

I support myself against the paperbark;
I rest for three days.

After resting, he made a *bull-roarer* and swung it violently, knocking down all the trees at that place. He began his journey, walking along and continuing to swing his bull-roarer. It struck boulders and broke them into fragments at a place called Goldjeman. These fragments were eagerly prized by the local people, as they made excellent stone knives.

Djamar continued walking, as celebrated in the song verse:

Straight I walk;
Straight in the hot season.

He went southward, continuously whirring his bull-roarer, then turned west and dived into the sea.

At a place called Ngamagun Creek he came ashore again and found there a bloodwood tree, which he split into short boards and made into *inma* boards of the bull-roarer kind. He straightened them by holding them over a *fire*, bored holes at one end for the *hair strings*, then tried them out by swinging them around. After that he pushed the boards (which were now sacred objects, *tjuringa* or *inma*) into the stony bed of the creek in such a way that they formed a straight line, then went back to the seashore and rested before continuing his journey.

Next he came to a place called Djarinjin where he felt under a rock and caught a rock-fish. The spikes of the fish pierced his arm and made it bleed. He plugged the vein with a wooden plug before returning to Ngamagun Creek. His wound began bleeding again and filled a stone basin. By his act, blood became a sacrament and the bleeding was enacted in ritual, accompanied by the song verse:

Sea cool, Djamar's *tjuringa* roars;
His life blood drops into the trough;
He replugs his wound.

Djamar then left his bull-roarer or *tjuringa* out on a *black* reef in the sea, where it still can be seen. He then carved another bull-roarer from a bloodwood tree with a yellow trunk. He swung it vigorously. The string broke and it whirled up into the sky where it came to rest in a black spot near the *Southern Cross*, which in this mythology is the realm of the dead. This is commemorated in the song verse:

The hair-string breaks;
Roaring a whirlwind whirls it on high.

There are other events and other cultural heroes associated with Djamar, as is usual in the mythology dealing with ancestral heroes. He had no father, nor did he marry, but had three sons from himself, who spread his message to other places. His mother was Gambad, which may simply mean the ocean from whence he came.

It is said that when Djamar walks quickly in the whirlwind a big grey dog is with him and that sometimes you can see the tracks of this giant dog. Djamar is equated with the *tjuringa* in the sky, but still watches his people to see that they obey the laws he set down for them. His myth and associated rituals and ceremonies were considered to be strictly for men and were not to be divulged to women.

Djang (*malagi; wunggud*) *Djang* means the energy stored in a sacred place. As *Bill Neidjie* says, 'Because that *Djang* we sitting on under, e watching that *Djang*, what you want to do. If you touch it you might get heavy cyclone, heavy rain, flood or e might kill some other place...other country e might kill im... We say *Djang*. Our lingo *Djang*. That secret place... Dreaming there.'

In a *Western Desert* language, this energy is called *malagi* and is compared to a spiritual power that maintains life and human existence. It is recharged by ritual activity. In this context *djang* or *malagi* places are energy sources and are like huge batteries from which life is generated.

See also *Auwa; Menstrual blood; Moipaka; Sacred places; Thalu places; Walkabout*.

Djambidji funeral ceremonies See *Ground carvings and sculptures; Hollow log coffins*.

Djambuwal See *Thunder Man*.

Djanggawul mythology and ceremonies The Djanggawul mythology, detailed in song cycles, underlies many of the ceremonies and provides motifs for the art of the *Duwa moiety* of the Yolngu people of *Arnhem Land*.

The ceremonies are called *nara* and are performed by the initiated men over several days. In preparation the men go out and prepare the sacred objects, which in this area are called *rangga*. These are wooden poles and posts kept hidden in *waterholes* or in the muddy banks and must be redecorated for the ceremonies.

Women have an important part to play in these initial ceremonies. They make long feathered strings which are then ritually stolen from them by the men. This relates directly to an incident in the myth which tells how once the ritual objects and ceremonies were owned by women, Djanggawul's sisters Bildjiwuraru and Miralaidj, but were stolen by men (see *Djanggawul and his two sisters myth*).

After the preliminaries are over, the ritual ceremonial ground is prepared and a shelter is erected. It now becomes a sacred area in which the Djanggawul will be manifest. The shelter symbolizes the womb of the two sisters of Djanggawul. The first *dances* relate to

the rising and falling of the surf and sound of the sea and symbolize Djanggawul's paddling across the sea to Port Bradshaw.
Throughout the dancing and singing of the song cycle, invocations
are made which connect the power of Djanggawul with those
creating the ceremony.

Much of the latter part of the ceremony dramatizes the stealing
of the sacred objects from the two sisters. The cycle of rituals and
ceremonies concludes with a ritual bathing in which the men, followed by the women and children, dance down to the beach and
plunge into the water. This may symbolize the Djanggawul returning to their island home.

Afterwards there follows the ritual eating of sacred cycad nut
bread which has been made by the women. The eating of the
bread creates a sacred bond of friendship between the partici-
pants: they become as one.

The ceremonies not only strengthen the bonds between the
different tribal groups, but also stress the continuity between
the present people, their ancestors and the future generations. The
fertility of the universe is enacted in ceremonies based on the seasonal rhythms, for example the wet season, which by its arrival
assures the germination of plant life and then by its withdrawal
symbolizes the essential death of life. All life and universal activities, including the songs and ceremonies, are cyclical. If the ceremonies are maintained, the cycle will be ever-repeated, thanks to
Djanggawul and his two sisters.

Djanggawul and his two sisters myth On the island of Baralku,
far out to sea, lived the Djanggawul. There were three of them:
Djanggawul, his elder sister Bildiwuwiju (or Bildjiwuraru), who
had many children, and his younger sister, Muralaidj (or
Miralaidj), who had just reached puberty. After a long time they
decided to leave their island home and come to Australia. In a
sense, they were like missionaries in that they loaded up their
canoe with sacred objects and emblems which they kept in a con-
ical mat basket. As they put out to sea, the *Morning Star* shone
above their island home.

They landed on Yelangbara beach near Port Bradshaw on the
coast of *Arnhem Land*, which because of this became a sacred
place for evermore. It is marked by a rock which is said to be their
canoe and there is a freshwater spring there which Djanggawul
made when he plunged his *mawalan*, his walking stick, into the
sand. The stick itself grew into a she-oak tree. Then they heard
the cry of a *black* cockatoo and, glancing up at the sand dunes, saw
the tracks of an animal. It was a goanna. Djanggawul named it
djunda. Then they began their travels across the land, naming

Book Title: Aboriginal Mythology

Author: Mudrooroo

Page # ____ **Clue:** _____

_____

Page # ____ **Clue:** _____

_____

Page # ____ **Clue:** _____

_____

Page # ____ **Clue:** _____

_____

Page # ____ **Clue:** _____

_____

Page # ____ **Clue:** _____

_____

Page # ____ **Clue:** _____

_____

Page # ____ **Clue:** _____

_____

Page # ____ **Clue:** _____

_____

Aboriginal mythology

Mudrooroo

places and animals and placing sacred objects in the ground for
future generations. They peopled the country as they went and
finally reached what would become Elcho Island.

One day, Djanggawul tripped over a creeper and accidentally
pushed his walking stick into the mud. Instantly the seas rose and
flooded the country, separating Elcho Island and the mainland.

The myth continues in like manner until it is told how some
men, the sons of the two sisters, stole their sacred emblems, their
songs and their ceremonies. When they discovered this, after dis-
cussing the theft, Bildiwuwiju and Muralaidj forgave their sons
because they still had their wombs, a visible sign of power which
men could never steal.

At last, after many adventures and the passing on of important
cultural artefacts, ceremonies, songs and even language, the
brother and his two sisters returned to their island home.

This corpus of myths is important in that, among other things,
it places the origins of much of Arnhem Land culture outside
Australia. The foreign influence is apparent when we contrast it
with the cultures of other parts of Australia and find marked differences—though in northern New South Wales and southern
coastal Queensland, it is said also that ancestral cultural heroes
came from overseas (the Three Brothers and their Grandmother),
and in the *Kimberley* region it is also told that the *Wandjina*, or at
least some of them, came from the sea; but in the inland areas
such as the *Western Desert*, the great ancestors sprang from the
land.

In this truncated version of the myth, many important events
and elements have been left out, such as the meeting with more
ancient indigenous *ancestral beings*. Other Arnhem Land song
cycles, which seem to be more historical than mythical, record the
visits of other peoples such as the Maccassans from Indonesia. It
is thus possible that the Djanggawul and his two sisters mythology records the ancient arrival of three cultural heroes who had
a great impact on the people and culture of Arnhem Land and
that as the events receded far into the past, they became myth-
ologized, as happens in other ancient spiritual traditions.

See also *Djanggawul mythology and ceremonies; Duwa moiety*.

Djingun See *Kimberley*.

Djinini See *Curlews; Mudungkala; Pukamani funeral ceremonies*.

Djuit See *Antares*.

Djurt-Djurt the nankeen kestrel See *Balayang; Bunjil; Crow*.

Doan the glider possum See *Two Brothers*.

Dogs (or dingoes) are said by archaeologists and others to be a
late arrival in Australia, arriving from Asia some thousand years
ago. This may or may not be true, although there is evidence in the
mythology for their arrival from offshore, but this occurred in the
Dreamtime and subsequently they became *ancestral beings* to many
Aboriginal groups, especially in the *Western Desert* and central
Australia.

The *elders* of the *Bunuba people* of the *Kimberley* region of
Australia relate a myth of the arrival of dogs in Australia. The
Melatji Law Dogs are said to have waded ashore at King Sound
after swimming across the Indian Ocean. From there they began
travelling towards the Napier and King Leopold Ranges. They
went as far as Fitzroy Crossing, then came back down to Windjana
Gorge, in their journey touching all the major water sources of the
country. They are thus linked with the water snake mythology.

The male dog was called Yeddigee and the female Lumbiella.
She had pups at Tunnel Creek, a famous haunt of the fighter
Jandamara. The elders of the Bunuba declare that the dogs finally
painted themselves onto the rocks at a place called Barralumma in
the Napier Range and that is where they still are.

But far to the east at Winbaraku in central Australia, the Melatji
dogs are found. They are associated with the giant snake creator,
Jarapiri, who was blind and was carried along by other ancestral
spirits as well as the Melatji dogs north to a cave at Ngama, near
the Aboriginal town of *Yuendumu*.

Ngama is a sacred law place for the Walbiri people and is looked
after by their elders. Here the Melatji dog women gave birth to
puppies and the Melatji dog men drew the giant snake Jarapiri
from the *earth* and milked him of his knowledge. A large painting
commemorates this feat. The dog men carry Jarapiri triumphantly
on their shoulders. Jarapiri, the giver of law, culture, ceremonies,
weapons, tools, songs and stories to the many Aboriginal communities associated with this *Dreaming*, is thus linked to faraway
Kimberley in the extreme north of Western Australia.

Still further east, from the Mingunburri group of Bundjalung
people who live just across the borders of New South Wales and
Queensland at the headwaters of the Albert river, Christmas
Creek and Running Creek, there is the myth of two dogs. In their
territory stands the fortress-like Mount Widgee, a sacred place of
the two dogs.

The myth associated with this sacred place concerns two men, Nyimbunji and Balugaan, and two dogs, Burrajan the male dog and his bitch Ninerung. These dogs chased a kangaroo to a place called Ilbogan, where it jumped into the lagoon there and was changed into a water snake. They began their trek home to Mount Widgee, but on the way home were caught by the local people who began to cook them. Nyimbunji and Balugaan had gone looking for their dogs and saw the smoke of the cooking fire. They took revenge on the killers of their dogs, then put the dogs' corpses in bark shrouds and carried them home to the mountain, but pieces of the corpses dropped off at various places along the route. At Mount Widgee, they took the remains of the dogs to the waterfall at the head of Widgee Creek, where they turned into stone, one falling east and the other west. It was believed that the dogs came alive every night as giant dingoes and roamed around the area. The mythology of *giant dogs* is extensive and stories are found all over Australia.

A variant of this myth is told in *Cape York peninsula* in the far north of Queensland. Here, the two dogs belong to an old woman.

The shape of the Lemington range as seen from the flat coastal plains of the Gold Coast of southern Queensland is in the shape of a dog. I was shown this when I was there.

Among my people, the *Bibbulmum*, elders relate the story of two dogs, a male and female, who travelled north from Albany. They came across two men and ate them. After a time, they felt the men scratching and fighting to get out from their stomachs. They vomited them up and the men turned into a white stone, like a huge snake's egg. After this the dogs became mad with thirst and separated to find water. The male dog went north-east, while the female dog went south-west and found water. She dug a hole in the ground at a place called Nyeerrgoo, which became a permanent source of water for the Bibbulmum. It the old days the water could only be approached if one went naked. Once divested of all clothing, a person had to go along the tunnel which the dog made in her quest for water, then strike the water with a hand and fill a vessel made from bark. If a person entered the cave clothed, it is said that the water would rise to drown them, or the spirit of the female dog would howl at the offender until he or she died.

See also *Bundjalung nation. Parachilna.*

Dolphins The dolphin is a symbol of the *Gold Coast*, the resort area of southern Queensland and an important ancestor, Gowonda, of *Aboriginal* people of southern Queensland.

Oodgeroo, elder of the Noonuccal people of Queensland, told me the story of how dolphins used to be friends of humankind and helped them in their fishing. They used to drive shoals of fish into the shallow waters so that the people could gather them up. The Noonuccals of Minjerribah (Stradbroke Island) had a system of sounds, a language by which they could talk to the dolphins. Some of the British invaders hid and listened to these sounds and used them to get the dolphins to drive the fish into the shallows, but unlike the *Aborigines* they also caught and killed the dolphins. Because of this they stopped coming and have only recently returned.

Dolphins are also important on Groote Eylandt off the north coast of Australia. The myth, as told by the *elders* of the Wanungamulangwa people who inhabit the island, relates how the earliest ancestors of the Wanungamulangwa were the dolphins, the Injebena, who lived and raised their families in the deep waters between Chasm and Groote Islands.

See also *Great battles*.

Domjum See *Yagan*.

Dooloomi See *Tooloom Falls*.

Dorabauk Dorabauk was a famous *Koori* shaman of the late nineteenth century who once brought a man back to life. He was called to cure an ill person and when he arrived at the camp he found the patient on the verge of death. Dorabauk at once set out after the departing soul and after a time returned with it wrapped up in a rug. He said that he had flown to the very edge of the *Earth* and captured the soul just as it was about to ascend into the sky. He put the soul back into the man, who subsequently recovered.

Dreaming Dreaming, in the sense of dreams, or the state between waking and deep sleep, is a state when revelations or instructions are received from the ancestors. Thus myths, songs and ceremonies are received in this state. This is the literal meaning, for the concept of Dreaming has been expanded into a deep spiritual and metaphysical concept, and in fact Dreaming and mythology may be seen as one and the same thing: the deep mental archetypes and wisdom images which we receive to guide us when the conscious mind is placed in a state of quiescence. Dreamings are those archetypes symbolized as *ancestral beings*, who came before and continue to live on in the present generations. These eternal archetypes, sometimes equated with *totems*, are part of the spiritual identities of *Aboriginal* people.

Groups of people with the same Dreamings are sets of people bonded by a common link to the spiritual. Thus the *Nyungar* Dreaming, the *Wagyal*, is connected up with other snake Dreamings across Australia. The snake archetype or Dreaming is the fount of all magical power and wisdom and thus is the Dreaming dreamt by the shaman and the archetype from whom he or she derives healing powers.

Dreamings or totems are eternally present, although a foundation may be made and this is termed the *Dreamtime*, the beginning of the world. It was then that the ancestral beings moved about, forming the landscape, creating the plants, animals and people, founding and teaching language, ceremony, laws and marriage rules and stabilizing the cosmic and human order. Dreaming is also termed 'the Law' in the sense of the Hindu concept of *dharma*, the process underlying the universe. One's Dreaming is one's Law.

See also *Ancestral beings; Creation myths; Dreaming tracks; Dreaming tree of life; Great battles; Sacred places; Totems.*

Dreaming tracks Dreaming tracks are the ancient *Dreamtime* roads along which the ancestors travelled, for example, an important *Dreaming* ancestor of my country, the *Nyungar* country of south-western Australia, is the *Wagyal*, a water snake deity. He travelled over the country creating features such as the lakes, hills and rivers, including the Swan on which Perth is situated. The long edge of the escarpment seen from Perth is said to represent his/her body. A sacred fertility place is on Mounts Bay Road at the old brewery site where the deity laid her eggs. *Bibbulmum* tribal women of that area received their babies there (see *Conception beliefs*).

See also *Song lines; Walkabout.*

Dreaming tree of life (Yaraando) The Dreaming tree of life is found among many groups of Australian *Aborigines* and was symbolized in the great ceremonies held in the *boro circles* in which a tree was planted with its roots in the air to show that it grew in the *sky world*. It is recorded that during the ceremony *shamans* would ascend the tree and vanish, then return to exhibit many marvels.

There is a *Koori* story from Victoria of how in the *Dreaming* their ancestral spirits would go up into the sky by means of a giant Dreaming tree. Only the older, fully initiated men were allowed to do so. One day the taboo was broken by a young man who had lent his six hunting *dogs* to his brothers to go hunting in the sky world. That night, he noticed that there were only five dogs remaining. His brothers, unable to catch anything, had eaten the other dog. The young man decided on revenge and drilled a hole in the taproot of the giant dreaming tree into which he stuffed a live coal which slowly burnt through the root. The next day the other brothers climbed the giant tree to hunt, then, as they were ready to descend, there was a great crack and the tree fell. This myth is etched in the heavens. The trapped brothers may be seen as a cluster of stars and the top part of the tree, which was wrenched away from the tree as it fell, is now a *black* patch in the *Milky Way*.

In Victoria, in the Wimmera district, are travertine lumps which are said to be the seed cones of the giant tree and there is a depression by the Richardson river where the giant trunk came crashing down. Lake Buninjon marks the great hole where the roots were burnt.

See also *Matchwood tree; Southern Cross; Tree between Heaven and Earth*.

Dreamtime (or the Creation Time, the Altjeringa or the Tjukurrpa or *palaneri* time) The Dreamtime, the time of creation, symbolizes that all life to the *Aboriginal* peoples is part of one interconnected system, one vast network of relationships which came into existence with the stirring of the great eternal archetypes, the spirit ancestors who emerged during the Dreamtime.

At the beginning, when the *Earth* was a featureless plain or, in some myths, covered with water, these archetypes, our creative ancestors, in many shapes and forms, stirred and found themselves in the void, the featureless landscape, the waveless ocean. Some, like the giant serpents who had been sleeping under the ground, pushed upward and writhed across the void, creating as they went along the landscape in which we live today. Other ancestors descended from the sky or came from the sea and when they reached the land they commenced their work of creation, not only making all things but naming them. The creative ancestors are responsible for everything there is, including the laws, customs and *languages* which order the different Aboriginal *tribes* and communities.

The creative period of the *Dreamtime* is as much metaphysical as an epoch in time. Aboriginal people can bring into present the *djang*, the spiritual energy of those times, by engaging in rituals which the ancestors taught and connecting up with them. They believe that the spark of life, the soul which energizes them, is part of that ancestor, so by stimulating that part through ritual and ceremony a breakthrough can be made into the timeless time of the *Dreaming*, when all things are made and continue to be made.

See also *Ancestral beings; Creation myths; Dreaming*.

Droemerdeener See *Tasmanian creation myth*.

Druk the frog See *Southern Cross; Two Brothers*.

Dua moiety See *Duwa moiety*.

Dugul sisters See *Great corroborees*.

Dumbi the owl See *Great flood*.

Dundalli Dundalli is a hero of the people of Queensland. He belongs to one of the *tribes* which owned the land on which Brisbane, the capital of Queensland, now stands. He fought for his land and the invaders executed him by hanging in 1845.

The Duwa moiety The Duwa (or Dua or Dhuwa) moiety is one of the two great divisions of the Yolngu of *Arnhem Land*. It has ancestral cultural heroes who arrived by sea, while the other moeity, the *Yiritja* moeity, has ancestral heroes who came from the land.

According to the late Jack Mirritji, who passed on some of the cultural knowledge about his Yolngu people, the Brolga is the bird of the Duwa moeity and the Jabiru bird is that of the Yiritja moeity. It is a rule that Jabiru people can only marry Brolga people. The interrelatedness of both moieties can be seen in the initiation ceremony, where if a Duwa person is to be initiated, then the Yiritja moeity must act as overseers of the ceremony and ensure that good order be kept, and vice versa. Jack Mirritji tells us what this division means or should mean. He says that since Yolngu people are in a system of interrelationships, then everything a person owns belongs to everybody else as well. Everything is shared—a person's house, his food and belongings.

The *Djanggawul and his two sisters myth* is the underlying theme of the ritual life of the Duwa moeity, especially in their *nara* ceremonies. In these ceremonies the epic journey of the Djanggawul from the island of Bralgu to the coast of Arnhem Land is enacted, also their subsequent journeys on the continent. The ceremonies culminate in the ritual handling of the sacred objects, *rangga*, brought to Australia by the *ancestral beings*.

See also *Gunabibi ceremonies; Red ochre*.

Duwoon (Glennie's chair) Duwoon is an important Bundjalung
sacred place where the *bull-roarer* was given to the people for use
in ceremonies.

The story associated with the place is this. A grandmother and
her grandson were travelling from the mountains to the seaside,
and the boy stopped at a tree to cut out grubs (*djubera*). The
grandmother continued walking and left the boy behind. The boy
continued cutting out grubs and every chip the boy cut would fly
up with a roaring noise. By this he knew that the place was a
strong place, a *djang* place, and so he chopped off more chips and
put a cord on the ends to make them bull-roarers or *wobblegun* (the
Bundjalung word for bull-roarer). Even today you can hear the
bull-roarers sounding there.

Bull-roarers amongst the Bundjalung people were only touched
and used by men. They were used in initiation ceremonies and
were considered the voice of the ancestors. They were used to con-
vey messages between the tribal *elders* and also to connect with the
spirit world.

See also *Bundjalung nation*.

Dyaydyu the kangaroo rat See *Great corroborees*.

E

Echidna

Eagle Eagle (known in eastern Australia as Eaglehawk) and *Crow* are important moiety birds. They were used to separate the *Adnyamathanha people* into two divisions, which were then further separated into sections, with various animals and birds being used as clan or section names.

The Adnyamathanha Crow *elders* have a myth which shows the oppositional tendencies and rivalries between the two divisions. In the *Dreamtime* there lived an eagle named Wildu who had two crow nephews both called Wakarla. As a type of All-Father, he was always telling them what to do. He told them what food they could eat and what food the elders could eat and, worse, his two wives, Mudu and Ngalyuka, Brown Hawk and Kestrel, were in a 'wrong way' relationship with him. They both belonged to his moiety and this was against the Law. Both Wakarla belonged to the opposite moiety and were in the right relationship to them, but they were still novices and could do little as he was their uncle.

Finally they decided on a plan to get rid of him. They went to a place called Ulkananha and made a fake stick-rat's nest. They took some leg bones of a kangaroo and sharpened them at one end. They stuck these in the nest with the points up, then went to their uncle and told him that they had found a rat's nest. Wildu came to the place and wanted to hit the nest with his club; but his nephews persuaded him to jump on it instead. He did so and the sharp bones went right through his feet, splitting them as they are today.

The Wakarla nephews took Wildu's wives and called all the animals and birds together for a great ceremony at the boro ground at Ipaathanha. Wildu pulled himself from the nest and landed on a hill. All the animals jeered him. He decided to leave them and went northwards to Yurdlawarta (Mount Flint) where he died. His feathers may be seen there as blocks of flint.

Meanwhile his wives had left the ceremony to come to find him. They found one of his feathers, then a bit of featherdown. Finally they found him. He was lying there dead, his feathers scattered all around. His wives picked up the feathers and stuck them back into his body. They tried to start him breathing. They pulled him up and blew on him as they did so. Then Wildu began to move and came back from the dead. He flew up into the air, saying that he was going to eat all the old women and children. His wives scolded him, but he took no notice. He landed on the hill as before and watched the dancers below, then saw a heap of rocks which hid the entrance of a cave. He told his wives to dig a tunnel from the east side into the cave so that they could lead all the birds and animals into the cave as he was going to raise a huge storm to punish his nephews. He told them to sleep at the front of the cave.

That night he raised the storm and all the animals and birds fled for safety into the cave. Wildu's wives slept at the entrance of the cave as he had told them to do. Then he built a huge *fire*. All the animals escaped, but the birds were trapped in the cave. The first birds to get out were cockatoos. They were able to keep away from the flames and smoke and thus stayed white. The magpies and *willy wagtail*s were closer to the fire and were badly burnt and that is why there is a lot of *black* on them. The crows, who were white before, were burnt to a crisp and that is why they are black.

After this the eagle flew off, telling them that they could have the country and still muttering that he would eat all the old women and children. So to this day no one trusts the eagle and crows fly around with him to make sure that he kills only to eat.

Eaglehawk See *Bunjil; Eagle; Eaglehawk and Crow*.

Eaglehawk and Crow In many parts of Australia, the *Aboriginal* communities are divided into two halves which are often equated with birds symbolizing the opposites, the Ying and Yang into which the universe is divided. Thus *Eagle*, in South Australia, or Eaglehawk, in eastern Australia, represents Day or Light and *Crow* represents Night or Shade, as in the Ying and Yang circle, although as in Ying and Yang, the two halves are complementary, for example marriage must take place across the moiety line and certain ceremonies cannot be performed unless both moieties are represented.

There is a creation story which explains the origin of the 'halves'. Once in the *Dreamtime* a mosquito was buzzing around the bush and as he buzzed he eventually transformed into a blowfly, then into a small bird and at last into Crow. Crow found himself alone and wanted a wife. At that time there were other *ancestral beings* which lived in the trees. He collected a lot of grass, heaped it up and set *fire* to it. The dense smoke rose into the tree-tops. He quickly sharpened the thigh bone of a kangaroo and stuck it in the ground with the sharp point upwards. He sang one of the tree beings to him, singing that he would catch it and break its fall. One of them jumped and was impaled on the sharp bone. When he tugged it free, he found that it had a deep bleeding wound. He then carried the creature to the grass fire and purified it by *smoking* it. The wound stopped bleeding and he saw that the creature was a female Eaglehawk. He took it to his camp and eventually they became the first Crow man and Eaglehawk woman, the primordial ancestors of the *Koori* moieties. From them came the marriage rule of cross-moiety marriage.

The story also sets the rule that women on reaching puberty had to be purified by smoking before they became eligible for marriage.

There are many myths concerning the wily Crow and the more phlegmatic Eaglehawk.

See also *Bellin-Bellin; Bunjil; Crow; Kimberley; Trickster character.*

Earth Earth, to many *Aboriginal tribes*, is the foundation of all life. Some, such as the *Nyungar*, see it as the *Great Mother* with the surface being her skin. Thus to pierce her skin is to wound her. As *Bill Neidjie* says, 'Earth...exactly like your father or brother or mother because you got to go to earth, you go to be ome to earth, your bone...because your blood this earth here.'

Also, to many Aboriginal groups the Earth is divided into male and female areas. Men will not venture into the female areas, or women into the male areas.

It may be said that almost all Aboriginal mythology is based on the earth from which many of the ancestors arose with the land-scape being a living story of their *Dreamtime* actions. In fact, earth and humankind are intimately linked, and if a person's country, over which he has custodianship, is injured, then the person becomes sick and dies.

See also *Ancestral beings; Cosmography; Djang; Earth, water, fire and air; Great Mother; Sacred places; Thalu places; Underworld.*

Earth, water, fire and air The elements of *earth*, water, *fire* and air lie at the heart of many *Aboriginal* myths. Earth is the first element, from which water must be liberated, then water is the second element, from which fire must be taken, and the smoke of the fire represents air. The first two are usually female, and males enter them at their peril, or the male *ancestral beings* are born from them; the second two are male and are used in male rebirthing techniques in the *boro circles*, though in myth fire was often once owned by women from whom it was stolen (see *Crow*). It partakes of both sexes, and thus in the male rebirthing ceremonies the male initiate must pass through fire to be then purified by smoke.

See also *Red, black, yellow and white.*

Echidna The echidna is connected with water in the mythology of many *tribes*, thus he is sometimes associated with the freshwater turtle.

In one story, once there was a shortage of water and all the animals were dying of thirst except Echidna, whom the other animals suspected had a secret water supply. Bimba-towera the finch was told by the other animals to watch Echidna. He did so, but Echidna realized it. He said nothing, but burrowed into the *earth* with his strong claws. Finch put his head in the tunnel, but the ceiling collapsed and he withdrew in alarm.

After his failure, Tiddalick the giant *frog*, a being also strongly associated with water, offered to help. Once in the *Dreamtime* he had swallowed all the water and had been forced to disgorge it. He was much more wily than Finch and finally saw Echidna go to a large flat stone. When he lifted it, Tiddalick darted across and dived into the depression beneath. It was filled with water. He let out a loud croak and the other animals rushed up. They threw Echidna into a thorn bush, then slaked their thirst.

In memory of this occasion Echidna continued to have the thorns sticking from his back.

See also *Frog; Great corroborees.*

Eclipse of the moon The eclipse of the *moon* was an omen which meant that someone on a journey had met with a serious accident.

Eclipse of the sun The eclipse of the *sun* meant that someone was working *black* magic on someone.

Eelgin See *Giant dogs*.

Elders Most *Aboriginal* groups in the old days were guided in their day-to-day activities and spiritual duties by the older men and women. Today, in most communities, elders are held in great respect as repositories of knowledge.

Emu The emu is prominent in *Aboriginal* mythology and in some accounts emus are the seven sisters who became the *Pleiades*.

Among the *Koori* people of Victoria the emu was associated with the native companion bird, and in the corpus of myths about the origin of the *sun* the emu and the native companion are the cosmic actors who bring light to the *Earth*.

The *elders* of the *tribes* living along the *Murray river* told how in the *Dreamtime* there was no sun and the people only had the faint light of the stars as illumination. In the Dreamtime, emus were sky-birds and never touched the Earth; then once one of them swooped close to the Earth and saw that people were living there. On another occasion, she saw them dancing and singing. Emu could restrain herself no longer and for the first time ever landed upon the Earth and found herself among a group of native companions. She asked them if she too might live on the Earth. One of the native companions quickly hid her wings behind her back and told Emu that she could never live on the Earth because her huge wings would get in the way. They had to be cut off. Emu agreed, but when she was wingless, the native companion spread her own wings and flew off with her tribe, all laughing at the trick they had played on her. Kookaburra perched on a nearby tree also laughed at the trick and, when he remembers, continues to laugh at it to this day.

Emu adjusted to living on the Earth, however, and when the breeding season came built a huge nest which she filled with eggs and sat on. One day the native companion was out with her children and saw the emu sitting on her eggs. She decided to play another trick on her. She quickly hid her brood, except for one chick, went up to Emu and greeted her. The emu, who was somewhat stupid, bore her no malice, as she had grown quite used to living on the Earth. Native Companion saw the huge pile of eggs and declared what a worry it was to have so many children all at once. She pointed to her one chick and said that it was much easier with a single child to look after. She suggested that Emu break all her eggs except for one and the foolish bird followed her advice.

However, Gnawdenoorte, son of the All-Father, was watching and decided to punish the native companion. He caused her long and graceful neck to become crooked and wrinkled and her sweet beguiling voice to become a harsh croak. From then on, the native companion could only lay one or two eggs. This made her very bitter towards Emu, though it had been her own fault. In the next breeding season she came to Emu, but with her hideous wrinkled neck and harsh voice, she had lost the power to persuade Emu to do anything. So Native Companion then resorted to violence. She sprang over the emu and into her nest where she began smashing the eggs. Emu rushed at her, but without wings could not catch her. Native Companion simply flew up whenever the Emu came close. Finally, she held Emu's last egg in her claw as she flew up and threw it high into the air, hoping that it would smash when it fell. However it went up and up and into the *sky world*, where it fell onto a huge pile of wood which Gnawdenoorte had piled up there. The collision was so great that the wood burst into flame and the whole world was flooded with light. Gnawdenoorte saw how much better the world was with light, so each day he lights up another pile of wood.

Eora tribe The Eora *Koori* tribe were the traditional owners of the land on which Sydney, the largest city in Australia, now stands. The tribe was divided into various groups or clans such as the Kuringgai, Kameragal, Bidjigal, Borogegal, Buramedigal and Kadigal.

See also *Corroboree; Pemulwuy; Red waratah*.

Extinct giant marsupials Fossil bones of giant marsupials have been found in Australia and many *Aboriginal* groups have stories about the time of the giant animals. The Adnyamathanha *elders* have stories of the Yamuti, huge mammal-like animals either like a giant kangaroo or wombat which once roamed their country. It has been suggested that these might have been the extinct diprotodon.

Other communities tell of giant kangaroos and other animals. In southern Queensland, for example, there are tales of a giant man called a Yowie. He is said to be very hairy and to haunt the thick rainforests. He has been seen on various occasions, whereas amongst the Adnyamathanha it is said that only *shamans* could see the Yamuti, but now that skill is gone.

The *Diyari people* thought that the heavy bone fossils of the extinct marsupials were the bones of giant animals they called Kadimakara, who once roamed the *sky world*, gazed down upon the world beneath, became mesmerized by the large lakes of water there and fell to *Earth*.

F

Fire maker and fire totem

Finke River Mission See *Hermannsburg Mission*.

Fire Fire is often either given by or stolen from a female ancestor, symbolizing her warmth and light, by a male ancestor such as *Crow*. He then keeps it for himself and it has to be stolen from him or gained by trickery. Often the sign of the gaining of fire is marked on the body of the bird or animal, thus the blackness of Crow, who was burnt in the skirmish to gain fire for the good of everyone (see *Crow*).

There are many stories about fire, the stealing of fire and the first making of fire. In *Arnhem Land*, women were the possessors of fire and it was stolen from them by their sons, who became *crocodiles*. They in turn kept fire for themselves until it was stolen by the rainbow bird who gave it to everyone.

Amongst the *Wik Munggan* people, it is told that in the *Dreamtime* there was a man named Fire who alone knew how to make it. Once the men wanted to start a fire in order to drive game from the high grass. Fire agreed to make the fire for them.

He broke off two sticks. He put one down and made a small hole in it. Then he picked up the other stick, placed an end in the hole and began twirling it. He twirled and twirled and nothing happened. He tried another stick with the same result. He broke off a green stick and said, 'This will be the one.' He pulled out some grass, laid it down and put the spark he kindled into it. He blew on it and the grass caught fire. That is how Fire taught men to make fire by rubbing sticks together.

Fire and the products of fire are considered to have healing properties. The ashes of particular plants are rubbed on wounds and suffering parts of the body. Aromatic plants and flowers, together with green branches and leaves, are spread on top of a fire to form a platform on which a sick person is laid. The smoke and steam from the platform contain the healing properties. A friend of mine became ill with poliomyelitis when a child. He was taken to the *bulyaguttuk* (shaman) who smoked him over a fire on a platform of green branches and plants and he was cured.

See also *Eagle; Earth, water, fire and air; Mundungkala; Shamans; Trickster character; Willy wagtail; Wudu ceremony of the Kimberley*.

First man child Children are said to be found at fertility places. The *Wik Munggan elders* narrate a myth concerning the creation of the first man child and the subsequent fertility place. Once in the *Dreamtime* a single man came from the West and met a woman. They decided to stay together and then to make a baby. They made it of clay, using scarlet seeds for eyes, blades of grass for hair and string for the intestines. The man then placed this baby head-first into the vagina, then pushed through red gum from the bloodwood tree, followed by milky sap from the milkwood tree. He worked away at the vagina and eventually the baby became alive. It continued to grow and the woman's belly began swelling, as did her breasts. Now the baby moved and turned around.

The husband went off hunting and while he was away the woman gave birth. The head of the baby emerged first, then out came the red gum and the baby was born. The woman buried the afterbirth in a hole in the ground. The husband returned and found out that the baby was a boy. He looked after the mother. He dug *yams* for her which she ate and caught a small catfish for himself. He let the big ones go by unharmed. After a time the baby's skin darkened and the navel cord became dry and broke off. The woman took this to the man. She collected yams and small fish, smeared clay on her forehead and also rubbed her breasts with clay. She put on a grass skirt, picked up the baby and painted its face with a white streak down its nose and rubbed charcoal over its body. Then she carried the baby to the father with roots and fish for him. He held the baby.

After this, as is the way in these stories, the three sank down into the *earth* to form a sacred *djang* place. The name of this place is Pukauwayangana, the boy baby fertility place. Men coming to the place will chase out boy babies and women will become pregnant.

See also *Childbirth; Conception beliefs*.

First woman The myth of the first woman is told by the *elders* of the Kalkan clan of the *Wik Munggan* people. *Moon* and *Morning Star* were originally two newly initated young men who came travelling from the north-east southwards across the land. This was in the *Dreamtime* and as yet there were no women. As they travelled they sang and made the rivers as they went along. The moon was the elder brother and the morning star was the younger brother. The elder brother made the younger do all the tasks which were eventually to become those assigned to women.

Once in their creative travels they lay down to sleep and during the night the elder brother got up and castrated his brother. He made a slit where the brother's genitals had been and squeezed his brother's chest to make breasts. That is the story of how the first woman came to be.

Flesh groups See *Kin groups*.

Flies A fly myth is narrated by the *elders* of the *Wik Munggan*. In the *Dreamtime*, there was once a fly man and his wife. They were camping at a place one day, when Tata the *frog* came to them. 'I've come for you,' he said. They replied that they were tired and would come with him next morning.

Next morning, they began their journey and collected honey on the way. They reached Tata's camping place and stopped there. Next day, they went for more honey. They asked the frog to mix it with water, but he refused. They asked him again and he refused again. They began to quarrel and fight. After wounding each other, they separated. It is said that in the fight, Tata the frog received a flat head and the fly a *black* face and body from being attacked with a firebrand by Tata.

The man and his wife went back to their place and descended into the *earth*. The man, before going into the earth, said, 'This is the fly's sacred place. Henceforth, when people come here and chase away the flies and thus awaken me, I will send flies into their eyes so that their eyes will become swollen.'

Flinders Range Flinders Range is in the country of the *Adnyamathanha people*, north of Adelaide, the capital of South Australia. A large portion of it has become the Gammon Ranges National Park.

The Adnyamathanha *elders* have a story to explain the creation of the Flinders Range. Long ago the whole country was flat and there was a kangaroo named Urdlu and a euro named Mandya who travelled around the plain. They had a special food, the wild pear root which they named *ngarndi wari*. Urdlu used to find lots of food and Mandya little. Once the euro came to the kangaroo and begged him for some food. He gave him some and the euro found it delicious. They went to sleep and next morning Mandya followed the kangaroo's tracks until he found where he had got the food from. Urdlu awoke, found him gone from the sleeping place and in turn followed his tracks. When he found him he gave him a good beating. The euro went off by himself and lay down to sleep. His hip started to hurt and he reached down and pulled a pebble from the sore. He blew on it and instantly hills came up from the plain. The more he blew the more hills came up. Urdlu looked and saw the hills coming up. The kangaroo is a plains animal and he became afraid that he would have no home, so with a sweep of his tail he swept the range of hills back where they are today.

See also *Akurra serpent; Arta-wararlpanha; Madkandyi the Terrible Whirlwind; Parachilna; Western Desert.*

Floods Floods are a frequent occurrence in Australia and they feature in may myths.

The cause of the Tambo river flooding in Victoria is ascribed to Kaboka the thrush. Once, it is related, Kaboka went hunting and only managed to kill one single miserable little wallaby. However, as is the *Aboriginal* custom, he prepared to cook it and share it with the others. They took one look at the skinny carcase, sniffed it and said that they would not eat it. This made Kaboka very angry. He took it back and told them to find their own food. Then he lit a sacred *fire* and began a ceremony, dancing around it until he raised a terrible storm and the rains began. He kept on dancing and the rain kept on falling until the water spread across the country and drowned his companions. Today, when the Tambo river is in flood, it is because Kaboka is remembering that episode and is dancing around his sacred fire.

See also *Baskets and bags; Frog; Gondwanaland; Great battles; Great flood; Rain-making.*

Flying foxes Flying foxes are a quarrelsome family, always squealing and snarling as they hang upside-down on the branches of trees, hiding by day in the thick scrub and waking at night to plunder fruit trees. They are credited with the invention of the first spear thrower, a device similar in shape to the leg and claw by which flying foxes hang upside-down.

Their quarrelsome nature is shown in a myth of the *Wik Munggan*. In the *Dreamtime*, the red flying foxes were men. They used to fasten the nose of their spear throwers with gum and, cutting a bailer shell, would stick the pieces on with beeswax. They used a small spear, a pepin with a wooden point and no barb. They also cut acacia wood, whittled down the four wooden prongs and fastened them to the hilt with gum. They shaped barbs from bone, planing them on a flat palette, then fastening them on with string made from the fibre of the fig tree. They smeared their *spears* with red clay and painted on *white ochre*, or pipeclay, with the finger. Then they carried them on their shoulders.

Once when they were quarrelling, they began throwing their spears and speared Mukama, a *black* flying fox. He was speared by a red flying fox named Wuka, who said that he might spear him in the thigh as payback. Mukama did so and killed him. Wuka was laid in a hole and they burnt him in an earth oven, laying tea-tree bark over the top and covering it all over with sand. This is the way flying foxes are cooked today. They stood posts about the grave, on the top of which they placed jabiru feathers, in the middle *emu* feathers and at the base jabiru feathers again. They laid emu feathers all around and left him there.

The killing of Wuka began a vendetta in which one of the black flying foxes was killed. They dug a hole, buried and burnt him, then set up two poles over him, one at the head and the other at the foot. The vendetta continued until they all sank into the ground.

Thus began the species of flying foxes. The place where the flying fox ancestors went into the ground became a waterhole. People hit the water with the flat of their hands and say, 'Let there be plenty of flying foxes everywhere.'

Fogarty, Lionel See *Cherbourg Aboriginal settlement*.

Fomalhaut The Fomalhaut star was believed by the many *Koori tribes* to be the *moiety ancestor* Eaglehawk (see *Eaglehawk and Crow*).

Freshwater turtle See *Echidna*.

Frog Frogs are associated with water and in dry arid regions in times of scarcity of water, there is a frog which gorges itself with water then buries itself into the ground and waits, perhaps for years, for the next rainfall. The *Aboriginal* people know this and when there is a drought, they dig them up for water.

The frog has entered mythology as a great drinker of water and once it is related he drank up all the water in the world. There are a number of *Koori* myths about Tiddalick the frog; here are a couple.

This is the account of the Kurnai Kooris of Gibbsland, Victoria. Once Tide-lek (Kurnai spelling of Tiddalick) had been sick and drunk so much water that he had drunk up all the water in the world. There was none left for anyone else. Tide-lek wanted to relieve the others' suffering, but could not bring up the water. Finally, it was decided that one way of making him disgorge the water was by making him laugh. Everyone tried and failed. At last No-yang the eel began to *dance* on his tail, and wriggled so much that Tide-lek laughed. All the water gushed from his mouth and caused a flood in which many were drowned. Others escaped by taking refuge on high ground.

Borun the pelican decided to save the survivors. He made a large canoe, rescued the marooned groups and brought them back to the mainland. On one island, he found a female he wanted as his wife. However, she was frightened of him, so she wrapped a log in her possum skin rug and placed it near the *fire* so that it looked as though she was lying there asleep. When Pelican came, he called out to her, received no reply, felt the possum skin rug and found the log of wood. Beside himself with lust and anger, he decided to avenge himself on everyone. He began daubing himself with *white ochre*, but as he was doing so, he turned into stone and is now White Rock, the northernmost islet in the Seal group, about eight miles south-east of Rabbit Island, east of Wilson's Promontory. Before this all pelicans were *black*, but now they are black and white, owing to the pipeclay their ancestor used.

In eastern Australia there is a similar myth about Tiddalick the giant frog. In the beginning, the *Dreamtime*, there was no water, and everything was dying of thirst. All the waters were contained in Tiddalick the giant frog. The ancestors came together to discuss how to bring water into the world. They knew that Tiddalick had swallowed all the water. How to release it? They decided that he had to be made to laugh. A worm ancestor tickled him and Tiddalick opened his mouth and his body shook with laughter. Out came the waters, and filled the rivers, streams, billabongs and *waterholes*. The creatures happily quenched their thirst and vegetation began growing. The Giant Frog laughed and laughed, so much so that he lost his voice. It became a hoarse croak and today this reminds the *Kooris* of the time when the *earth* was parched and dry.

See also *Echidna; Flies; Great corroborees; Southern Cross; Two Brothers*.

G

Great snake Jarapiri

Gaiya See *Giant dogs*.

Galaxy The galaxy is said by the Wotjobaluk *Koori* people of Victoria to be the smoke of the campfires of the ancestors. The dark spot near the *Southern Cross* is the place where the giant *Dreaming tree of life* was fastened and enabled men to ascend to the sky world.
   See also *Stars and constellations*.

Galiabal See *Bundjalung nation*.

Gallerlek See *Aldebaran*.

Gambad See *Djamar*.

Gammon Range National Park See *Flinders Range*.

Gayandi See *All-Fathers*.

Gender roles Gender roles are a part of *Aboriginal* culture, for
one of the Aborigines' all-abiding dualities is that between man
and woman, more or less symbolized in the woman as gatherer,
man as hunter, although it goes back to a basic model of woman
as childbearer or womb-bearer and man as barren, unable to bring
forth life.

During her fertile years woman is connected to the cycles of the
Earth. Her role and disposition are identical with the functions of
the Earth: life-giving, nurturing, healing, maintaining and giving
service to living things. Women and Earth are one and, unlike
men, are life-givers and protectors. The role of men differs, pre-
cisely because they have no womb and no natural blood flow. This
means that the men must get in touch with the great mysteries
and energies of life through ceremonies. To remain in touch with
the fecundity of nature, a man must develop and keep in contact
with a more abstract spirituality, symbolized by the great archetypes, in order to maintain his connection to the natural and
creative processes.

See also *Earth; Earth, water, fire and air; Gunabibi ceremonies;
Initiation process; Menstrual blood; Sun; Yams*.

Gertuk the mopoke See *Two Brothers*.

Giant dogs The mythology of giant *dogs* is found all across
Australia and there is one story from the far north of Australia,
Mornington Island off *Cape York peninsula*, which has been related
by *Dick Roughsey* of the Lardil people. He published a children's
version of the same myth under the title *The Giant Devil Dingo*.
Dick Roughsey related how the dog came west to Cape York and
Mornington Island and said that there were two dog *Dreamings*,
one on Mornington Island itself and the other on the smaller
Denham Island. His version differs from the myth found on the
mainland.

In Dick Roughsey's version, an old grasshopper woman, Eelgin,
came from the west with the giant dog Gaiya. They both hunted
humankind for food. Once when Gaiya was out hunting two
young men, butcherbird brothers came to the old woman's camp.
They spoke to Eelgin, before becoming alarmed and running off.
Gaiya returned and the old woman sent him after the two butcherbird brothers. He followed their tracks, loping after them with
giant strides, across Cape York peninsula, drawing nearer and
nearer.

Finally the butcherbirds decided to ambush the giant dog at a place called Bulinmore, a big rocky pass through the hills. The dog came along and behind him came the old grasshopper woman, hobbling along with a stick. The butcherbirds began spearing Giaya and kept on until he was dead. They then called for all the people of the country to come and have a meal of cooked dog, then cut off the tip of his tail (in which his spirit resided) and sent it back to the old woman. The angry spirit bit Eelgin on the nose before the butcherbirds came down and killed her. They then sent her spirit to a place near Barrow Point, where she became a large rock. The marks that Gaiya's spirit made when biting her can be seen on the noses of all grasshoppers.

The body of the giant dog was divided up and the shaman, Woodbarl the white cloud, asked for the kidneys, the head and all the bones. Later he took the bones and also the skin to the top of a mountain where he made two small dogs which would be friends of humanity.

In the mainland version, as related by Tulo Gordon of the Guugu Yamidhirr people, the butcherbird brothers are replaced by the two magpie brothers and the old woman is replaced by a carpet snake, and thus connects up with the Melatji dog myths across the continent in the *Kimberley* region of Western Australia. The magpie brothers do not kill the giant dog or the carpet snake, but simply forbid them to kill human beings. The lonesome howl of the dingo is a cry of repentance for the killing and eating of human beings.

See also *Djamar; Parachilna*.

Gidabal See *Bundjalung nation*.

Gigu-Almura See *Cape York peninsula*.

Gigu-Imudji See *Cape York peninsula*.

Gigu-Warra See *Cape York peninsula*.

Gigu-Yalanji See *Cape York peninsula*.

Gin-Gin See *Mornington Island*.

Ginibi, Ruby Langford (1934–) Ruby Langford Ginibi was born at Box Ridge Mission, Coraki, in northern New South Wales and is an elder of the Bundjalung people. She has written a number of books and her best known work is *My Bundjalung People* (1994).

See also *Bundjalung nation.*

Glennie's chair See *Duwoon.*

Gneeanggar the wedge-tail eagle See *Sirius.*

Gnawdenoorte See *All-Fathers; Emu.*

Goanna Headland See *Australian indigenous mythology; Bundjalung National Park.*

Goanna the monitor lizard See *Bundjalung National Park; Canoes; Djanggawul mythology and ceremonies; Great battles; Great corroborees; Pea Hill; Yugumbir people.*

Gold Coast (Nerang) The Gold Coast in southern Queensland is in Bundjalung country and the signs of the travels of their ancestors are still prevalent today. Burleigh Heads, for example, is where one of the three brothers, Yar Birrain, landed (see *Bundjalung nation*).

There are important places sacred to the dolphin *Dreaming* along the coastline. The cultural hero, Gowonda, a great hunter and trainer of hunting *dogs*, became a white-finned dolphin, together with his dogs, and looked after humans by driving fish into the nets of the people. He can be identified by his white fin, which is the sign of a leader among a group of *dolphins.*

Goolaga See *Mumbulla state forest.*

Goolbalathaldin See *Roughsey, Dick.*

Goonana See *Mornington Island.*

Gondwanaland Gondwanaland was once a huge southern landmass consisting of Australia, New Guinea and parts of Indonesia. There are many myths of *great floods* across Australia which sank different parts of Gondwanaland under the sea. These may refer to the rising of the seas at the end of the last ice age thousands of years ago.

David Mowaljarlai equates Australia with a giant human body and calls it Bandaiyan. The mythic continent is full and rounded, unlike the Australia of today, parts of which are islands. Perhaps it refers back to the ancient Gondwanaland, before the rising of the seas.

See also *Great flood; Yarra river and Port Phillip*.

Gowonda See *Dolphins; Gold Coast*.

Grasshouse mountains The Grasshouse mountains north of Brisbane lie in the country of the Nalbo people. The story of their creation is that once the warrior Tibrogargan saw the ocean beginning to rise. He collected his children and led them away into the mountains and sent one of his sons, Coonowrin, to help his mother, who was pregnant. The boy ran away, and Tibrogargan was so angry that he smashed him on the head with his club and dislocated his neck. This incident remains in the landscape as Grasshouse mountains. There Coonowrin stands with his crooked neck and beside him is his mother, Berrwah, awaiting the birth of her child.

Great battles Aboriginal life is based on dualities such as moieties and other divisions such as light and shade, the intensity of *red ochre* and the passivity of *white ochre*. This is shown in the corpus of mythological stories which feature great battles between two antagonists or groups.

Many mythological battles occur in the *Dreamtime* and result in the reordering of the Dreamtime world into the present world. The Dreamtime, instead of being a static period, was a time of great change, as one cosmic age was replaced by another.

One great battle, it is related by the *elders*, took place at the mouth of the Logan river in Bundjalung country, northern New South Wales, between the ancestors of the *earth*, air and water creatures. Yowrgurraa the goanna was leading the land creatures in the battle and he was armed with a spear. The air creature Sparrow Hawk swooped down and snatched the spear, then flew over the waters and drove the spear into the back of Dolphin. Dolphin blew the spear out with a mighty blast and a torrent of water and blood flowed from the wound and flooded the land. This resulted in the islands, swamps, channels and creeks at the mouth of the Logan river and far south to the present-day town of Broadwater.

Another example is the great battle at *Uluru*, the large

rock monolith in central Australia, which marked the end of Dreamtime.

See also *Yugumbir people*.

Great corroborees Tulo Roberts of the Guugu Yimidhirr people of *Cape York peninsula* relates the myth of the great corroboree or series of ceremonies which occurred in the *Dreamtime*. It is a peaceful counter to the *great battles* which occurs in other myths.

In the Dreamtime all the creatures of the *earth* and water came together for a great series of ceremonies, but they picked an area which had no water and after three or four nights they began to feel very thirsty. They searched for water and found none.

Only the two turtle sisters, the Dugul sisters, did not join in the search. They had a secret supply of water and used to sneak off and quench their thirst. The other dancers noticed them sneaking off and set spies to watch them. They sent Dhagay the sand goanna, they sent Balin-ga the porcupine or *echidna*, they sent Frilled Lizard, then Carpet Snake. All failed. Finally, they decided on subterfuge and selected Walanggar the death adder to watch the sisters. He was successful. He saw the two turtle sisters poke each other in the chest, then drink their fill of the water which poured out. He told the others and they made plans. They decided to pick the best dancer. Burriway the *emu*, with his long legs, danced first, but he was not fast enough, then Kangaroo, Gadaar the wallaby, Gangurru the wallaroo and even old Balin-ga the echidna had a go, but they were all considered too slow. At last Dyaydyu the kangaroo rat was called on to perform. He began a shake-a-leg *dance* called Yimbaalu. He was judged the fastest and best, and the animals made plans for the next night's performance.

The next night, Dyaydyu lead the dancing while the two turtle sisters, as is the custom, sat with the women and joined in the clapping and singing. They sat right in the front row and Kangaroo Rat led a row of dancers towards them. When he came close, he suddenly leapt up and kicked the Dugul sisters right in their loins, one after the other. Water sprouted out from their bodies and flowed over the ground and kept on flowing until it had created lagoons, creeks and *waterholes* in every direction.

At the end of the corroboree, the sea and land animals exchanged skins. Crocodile and Goanna traded skins, for Crocodile wanted Goanna's tough skin because he lived in the water. Sea Urchin traded his hard spikes with Echidna or Porcupine, whose soft spikes were more suited to the sea. Even Ngawiya the big sea turtle traded shells with Land Tortoise, but Tortoise was in such a hurry to try on his new shell that he put it on back to front. Afterwards the creatures separated and returned

to their habitats and they remain there to this day.
    See also *Echidna; Frog*.

Great Father deities See *All-Fathers*.

Great flood Myths of great floods are found all across Australia.
The mythology of the people of *Kimberley* stress a great *Dreamtime*
flood which wiped out most of the population of the world. *Daisy
Utemorrah* tells of the time when the people were all drowned.
Long ago in the Dreamtime, a group of children began teasing
Dumbi the owl, a sacred bird connected to the *Wandjina*. They
tortured him, but at last he managed to fly away and to the
Wandjina where he complained of his treatment. The Wandjina
became angry and sent thunder and *lightning* and rain. The rain
fell and fell, and the waters rose and rose until all the people were
drowned, except for two children, male and female, who managed
to grab hold of the tail of a kangaroo and thus were carried to
higher ground. Daisy Utemorrah says that it was from these two
children that humankind continued.
    See also *Floods; Gondwanaland; Wullunggnari; Yarra river and
Port Phillip*.

Great Mother The Great Mother, to many *Aborigines* is the
Earth. To others she is *Gunabibi* or Kunapipi. She appears to have
been introduced to *Arnhem Land* from Indonesia when Indian
Tantric cults were introduced to Java and Sumatra and flourished
there for many centuries.
    See also *All-Mothers*.

Ground carvings and sculptures Ground carvings and sculptures are part of the ceremonies of certain *Arnhem Land* people as
well as the *Koori* people of southern Australia.
    In the Djambidji series of funeral ceremonies, the ground is
excavated in the shape of a boat in the centre of the boro ground
and the *hollow log coffin*, Badurra, is erected to stand within the
shape as if it was a mast of a ship. It is symbolic of the soul's journey across the seas to the *Island of the Dead*.
    In south-eastern Australia, the Kooris used carved and sculpted
ground designs in their elaborate boro man-making ceremonies.
The carvings included representations of reptiles, animals and
men and women as well as abstract designs. Huge earthen figures
of *Biame* were also moulded. Some of these figures were over 20
metres in length. The huge earthen figure was shown to the newly

made men by the *elders*, who explained his laws and the penalties for breaking them.

See also *Ground paintings; Rock engravings*.

Ground paintings The ground paintings of central Australia have been the inspiration for the modern acrylic paintings. Ground paintings are part of the religious ceremonies of the *Aboriginal* people.

First of all an area of ground is smoothed out and made ready. Sand, clay, ochres and other materials such as sticks, bird down, hair, plant fibre and blood are used to create the 'installation' which is a number of elaborate designs incorporating concentric circles, furrowed lines and raised sculptured forms. The designs represent the *ancestral beings* and their journeys and adventures.

See also *Bark paintings; Papunya Tula art; Rock paintings*.

Gubba Ted Thomas Gubba Ted Thomas is an important elder and custodian of the lore and traditions of the Yuin people of south-east New South Wales.

Gulibunjay and his magic boomerang This story is related by story-tellers at the *Yarrabah Aboriginal* settlement. Gulibunjay was a *Dreamtime* man who had a son, Wangal, who was a living *boomerang*. Once he threw the boomerang towards the ocean. It went around in a great curve and cut a path through the forest before swinging back to the ocean. It first hit a staghorn fern, then a red penda tree.

Gulibunjay followed along the great swathe cut in the forest by his son, the boomerang. He went along searching for his son and naming the various plants and animals and natural features of the landscape. When he came to the sea, he knew that his son had drowned, so he sat down on a mountain where he remains to this day, looking down at the sea and yearning for his son.

Gumbainggeri See *Bundjalung nation*.

Gunabibi (or Kunapipi) Gunabibi is an All-Mother deity, similar to the Greek goddess Demeter, whose cult and ceremonies have spread widely in northern Australia, crossing boundaries and encompassing peoples who speak different *languages*. The cult seems to have come from Asia via the Roper river, adding and adapting other indigenous ceremonies as it spread south.

The myth behind the Gunabibi is that of the *Wawilak sisters* who

were devoured by the giant serpent *Yulunggul*. This appears to
have been an indigenous myth which was adapted to the require-
ments of an imported cult of the *Great Mother*.

Gunabibi's overseas origin is stressed in one of the songs
devoted to her:

Tidal water flowing, white foam waves;
Rain water flowing into the river;
Paperbark trees; soft bark falls into the water;
Rain falling from the clouds;
Swirling river waters;
She emerges to walk on dry land.

See also *All-Mothers; Great Mother; Gunabibi ceremonies*.

Gunabibi ceremonies *Gunabibi* (or Kunapipi) is an All-Mother
deity who is the centre of an intensive corpus of rites and ceremonies. The sacred Gunabibi ceremonies are extremely secret
today, but from published accounts there appears to be linkages
with the Tantric cults of India, which in the sixth century AD
spread to Java and Sumatra and from there to *Arnhem Land*.

Gunabibi ceremonies are usually held in the dry season, when
food is plentiful, and can extend from two weeks to two months.
The ceremonial leaders are usually of the *Duwa moiety*. A *boro
circle* or ceremonial ground is prepared and when the ceremony is
ready to begin, a man swings a *bull-roarer*. This is the deep-
throated roar of the great serpent *Yulunggul* who came to devour
the *Wawilak sisters*. The ceremonial leader calls an answer and this
is followed by cries from the women in imitation of how the two
sisters cried out when they saw the giant snake approaching. Then
there are a number of rituals during which boys are passed
through the manhood ceremonies, until finally they are brought
into the boro ring to be taught *dances* by the men initiated into the
cult.

During the night, calls are exchanged between the men and the
women in the main camp. Eventually, the men take lighted torches
and dance towards the main camp where the women are hiding
under blankets, except for two old women who walk up and down,
detailing the foods forbidden to women at this time and also incidents from the mythology of the Wawilag sisters which refer to
women's business. Then a large hole is dug on the boro ground
into which men go and dance, signifying the animals, birds and
vegetables which fled when the Wawilak tried to eat them, and
eventually the swallowing of the two sisters is enacted out.

Two or three nights before the end of the ceremonies, the men sit around the *fires* in the boro ground and begin singing parts of the Gunabibi song cycle, and the women enter, some decorated with feathered string headbands. They dance the bandicoot dance, then leave and re-enter. The ceremonial leader of the women erects two objects. One is a post consisting of paperbark bound together with twine; the other is a pole decorated with *red ochre*. Then follows a dance which refers to the section of the myth where Yulunggul sent *lightning* while the sisters were in their hut. The lightning split a stringy bark tree. Pieces of this wood flew off and it was from them that the bull-roarer was made.

On the final night, the same dances are repeated and just before dawn, all the Duwa moiety men assemble at one end of the ceremonial ground and the *Yiritja* men at the other. All the men are painted with white paint and some carry *spears*. They dance towards each other. The bull-roarers roar and the women shrill from the main camp, then they go to the edge of the boro ground and make a shelter in which the birth of the child by the younger sister is mimed. After this the shelter is knocked down. Then, after having an image of the giant snake Yulunggul painted on their bodies for purification, the men are ritually smoked before returning to the main camp.

The Gunabibi ceremonies are an expression of the sacred mythology which releases the power invested in the *ancestral beings* and it is an important ritual in that women enter the sacred boro ground in their own right, in fact take the leadership to enact the time when ceremonies belonged to the women and not the men. The Gunabibi is as much the women's sacred ceremony as it is the men's, and this is apparent in the central place women's concerns or business has in it.

Gunya See *Barrier Reef*.

H

Hollow log coffin

Hair string Human hair string was used by the Australian *Aboriginal* people in many ceremonies. A hair string belt was worn by initiated men. In the old days, a *Bibbulmum* youth, on being initiated, was decorated with a human hair band and belt. These were visible signs that he had entered manhood.

See also *Trade; Waningga.*

Hare-Wallaby See *Winbaraku.*

Harney, Bill See *Idumdum.*

Healing fire See *Fire.*

Herbal medicines Any number of medicinal herbs and plants were and are still used by *Aboriginal* people all across the continent. It is not possible to list them all here and as far as I know no

Australian Aboriginal *materia medica* book exists.

In Victoria the *Koori* people used a multitude of herbs in a number of ways for healing properties: steaming, *smoking*, as infusions or teas, as poultices and vapour baths.

Gukwonderuk, old man weed (*Centipeda cunninghamii*), grows along the sides of creeks and rivers such as the Murray and is used for colds and chest complaints. Big bunches of the plant are gathered and boiled down. One or two teaspoons are taken and the amount is steadily increased to half a cup a day.

Mootjung or *burn-na-luk*, blackwood (*Acacia melanoxylon*), is used as a treatment for rheumatism. It is heated over a *fire*, then infused in water to bathe aching joints.

The aromatic leaves of *poang-gurk* or *tjapwurong*, river mint (*Mentha australis*), are crushed and inhaled for coughs and colds.

Taruk, small-leaved clematis (*Clematis microphylla*), is called the 'headache vine' and, as its name suggests, is used to relieve headaches.

Stinkwood and sandfly zieria (*Zieria arborescens* and *Zieria smithii*) are also used for headaches, the leaves either being bound around the head or crushed and inhaled.

Tjapwurong or river red gum (*Eucalyptus camaldulensis*) is a majestic tree, a grandfather tree with healing properties which may be absorbed by just sitting under it. Apart from this, its gum is used to shrink and heal burns and is mixed with water and taken as a cure for diarrhoea. Red gum leaves are also important in aromatic steam baths, a method of healing similar to the Native American Sweat Lodge.

Hermannsburg Mission Hermannsburg Mission or Finke River Mission, 120 kilometres south-west of Alice Springs, was founded by German missionaries in 1877 and was the home of the famous painter *Albert Namatjira* and the place where the painting of watercolours by the local *Arrernte people* developed into a fully fledged art movement.

The mission, by then a township, was passed into the control of the Arrernte people in 1980 and is now run by the Ntaria Council.

Missions such as these, although they did to a great extent inflict drastic changes on indigenous culture, also allowed many indigenous people to survive the killing times, when it was considered sport by the invaders to go out and kill our people. Often, like the fauna and flora, we were considered only vermin to be exterminated. The missionaries helped to alleviate the sufferings of those times, though we lost many important cultural beliefs and practices, owing to their influence and power.

Hollow log coffins Hollow log coffins were used by the *Aborigines* of *Arnhem Land* to intern the bones of their dead. These coffins, which stand upright, are elaborately painted with the ancestral spirits of the deceased.

The song and ritual of Hollow Log is the centrepiece of the elaborate Djambidji funeral ceremonies. Hollow Log is seen as firstly a dead tree, then as a coffin and lastly as a living, moving spirit being. It exists too as a humanly created artpiece, a memorial to the deceased person whose crushed bones lie within.

See also *Bark paintings; Ground carvings and sculptures; Honey; Tree between Heaven and Earth; Woijal.*

Honey Honey, which is found in hollow trees in the Djambidji song series of *Arnhem Land*, has come to symbolize the food of spirit beings who make their homes inside Hollow Log as it transforms itself from a dead tree into a coffin (see *Hollow log coffins*), then into a living spirit being, transferring the soul to the *Island of the Dead*. The bones of the deceased become the honey comb itself, and the honey comb and the flights of bees coming to it are signs of the generation and regeneration of all nature, a constant cycling and recycling of everything which exists.

See also *Crocodiles.*

Hydra To the Mara *Koori tribes* of Victoria the Hydra constellation is Barrukill, a great hunter of kangaroo-rats. On his right and a little above him are two stars. One is a kangaroo-rat and the other is his dog, Karluk. Above these are other stars forming a log. Underneath are stars forming his arm and his firestick. The dog chases the kangaroo-rat into the log which Barrukill sets fire to. He kills it as it tries to escape then eats it.

I

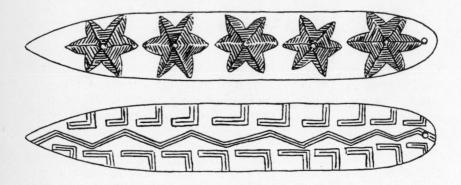

Inma boards

Idumdum (Bill Harney) belongs to the Wardaman country in the Northern Territory. He is a custodian of the esoteric lore associated with the *Lightning* Brothers and of the sacred site of *Ingelaladd*, 100 kilometres west of the town of Katherine. His father, Bill Harney (senior), wrote a number of books about the *Aborigines* of the Northern Territory.

Iga tree See *Adnyamathanha people*.

Ilara See *Universe*.

Injebena See *Dolphins*.

Inma boards *Inma* boards are sacred soul-boards of a number of desert peoples. They connect each individual to his ancestors and to the song and *Dreaming* lines of his country. Apart from this, *inma* boards are magic weapons. They come directly from the ancestors.

According to *Western Desert Aboriginal* communities, the long line of dark patches in the *Milky Way* between *Centaurus* and *Cygnis* represents the sacred *inma* board that the ancestors called the *Two Men*, *Wati Gutjara*, made and flung into the heavens as sung in the song verse: *'Pulina-pulina kaduana wanala rawu janani warai.'* *Pulina-pulina* refers to the dark patches of the Milky Way. A translation might go: 'Into the sky, a long way away journeys the *inma.'*

See also *Bull-roarer; Rangga; Tjuringa.*

Ingelaladd Ingelaladd is a sacred place, 100 kilometres west of the town of Katherine in the Northern Territory. It is where the *Lightning* Brothers descended into the *earth*. There are many rock art images here and images of the *ancestral beings* are imprinted in *red ochre* on the walls of a cave.

Initiation process The great initiation law ceremonies of male coming of age varied across the continent. Amongst the *Bibbulmum* it was a lengthy educative process during which the septum of the nose was pierced to signal a final stage in the process. Among other peoples, tooth evulsion and circumcision were practised towards the end of the ceremonies. Often the entire process took place over several years, during which time the initiate was taken across his land, usually by a maternal uncle who taught him the routes of the ancestors and the songs and stories detailing them. The initiation process is still important among many *Aboriginal* groups, though since the invasion there have been vast changes and the process has been considerably shortened.

In the northern parts of Western Australia the initiation process was particularly elaborate and began at the age of eight or nine when the boy went to stay in the unmarried men's camp. The first stage of initiation began when the older men—who may be grandfathers, fathers or maternal uncles, according to the kinship system—decided that it was time for the boy to be put through the law.

The process began with a ceremony during which a small pointed kangaroo bone was thrust through the septum of the boy's nose. Next morning the kangaroo bone was taken out and a turkey bone replaced it. The strict avoidance of women and girls began at this point. The second stage began when, without warning the boy, the guardian mixed up an ointment made from charcoal and fat and rubbed the boy all over with it. He then placed a band made of possum fur string around the boy's head. (In other areas, it was at this stage that one or more teeth were knocked out.) This second stage concluded with an evening ceremony.

Next morning the boy was taken by his guardian on a circular journey which lasted for some months and returned him eventually to the main camp. They stopped some distance away and the youth was rubbed with the charcoal and fat ointment, then the guardian added a little *red ochre* to his forehead and cheeks before painting his body with a design symbolizing his *Dreaming* ancestors. Finally, a possum fur string was placed around the boy's neck and under his right and left arm. His guardian and the other men from the camp decorated themselves and then conducted a ceremony at the boro ring.

Early next morning the boy's female relations cried over him before leaving him with the men. The guardian carried the boy off to a sacred shelter where he underwent the rite of circumcision. He had to stay there until he healed. After eight or nine days, he underwent a *smoking* ceremony. After the ceremony the men sang sacred songs while stamping the *fire* out, then ceremonies continued until the following morning, during which the youth received information only known to the initiated men. At none of these ceremonies were women and children or uninitiated men allowed to be present.

After several days the initiate passed through the law and was allowed to return to the men's camp as a full man, able to take part in men's activities and learn the important ceremonies and accompanying myths and songs. It was only after undergoing the process of going through the law, being made a full man, that he was allowed to marry.

See also *Gender roles; Kulama ceremonies; Moiya and pakapaka; Pearl shell ornaments; Pituri; Scorpio; Wollumbin.*

Inneroogun See *Dogs.*

Inwati See *Kulama ceremonies.*

Irwardbad See *Oobarr.*

Island of the Dead In many parts of Australia, including my own, there is a belief that there is a stopping place between the *Earth* and the *sky world* on an island.

For example, Ngurunderi the ancestor is said to have entered the sea near Kangaroo Island off the coast of South Australia (see *Sky world*). The souls of the dead followed this route by crossing first to the island to be purified before continuing their journey.

Among my people, the *Nyungar*, Rocknest Island, now a tourist resort, off the coast of Western Australia, is believed by many to be the Island of the Dead and many Nyungar still will not go there. When the Europeans first came to my country, we thought that they were spirits returned from the dead because they were the colour of dead bodies and came from the sea. They thus were called *djangara*, 'spirits' or 'ghosts'.

See also *Bralgu; Death; Ground carvings and sculptures; Honey; Morning Star.*

Ita the swamp-fish man See *Menstrual blood*.

J

Jirakupai the spear maker

Jabiru See *Duwa moiety*.

Jaknia See *Jirakupai*.

Jalgumbun (Mount Lindsay) Jalgumbun is a towering mountain in Bundjalung country said to be a resort of *shamans*. It is a place where the hairy spirit man, Njimbun, resides and he is easily moved to anger. The local *Aboriginal* people say that one should be careful if visiting the place not to anger Njimbun. People still see him there to this day.

Jandamara (*c*.1900?) Jandamara, also known as Pigeon, was an *Aboriginal* fighter of the *Bunuba people* who fought the invaders at the turn of the nineteenth century. He is also considered to have been a *maban*, or shaman. He could not be killed, as he kept his soul in his thumb—or big toe, according to another version— which had been dipped in the powerful waters of a sacred pool.

Eventually, he was betrayed and killed by being shot in the thumb (or toe).

Banjo Woonamurra, a Bunuba elder, is the custodian of the history of Jandamara's life.

Jangalajarra snake See *Pea Hill*.

Jarapiri The great snake Jarapiri was a creative ancestor and his exploits form the bedrock of most of the central Australian Walbiri people's mythology and ceremonies. Jarapiri belongs to the great corpus of snake myths found the length and breadth of the continent.

See also *Dogs; Rainbow snake; Walbiri creation myth; Yuendumu*.

Jarapiri Bomba See *Winbaraku*.

Jigara See *Bundjalung nation*.

Jinabuthina (Pompey) was a Diyari elder who in the late nineteenth century led the fight against the invaders of his country. He was shot when, at the head of 80 warriors, he attacked Umberatana station.

See also *Diyari people*.

Jindjiparndi people See *Burrup Peninsula; Ngarluma and Jindjiparndi peoples*.

Jinijinitch the great white owl See *Two Brothers*.

Jirakati the white-headed sea eagle See *Kulama ceremonies*.

Jirakupai The myth of Jirakupai is narrated on Bathurst Island. In the *Dreamtime*, that long-ago creative period, Jirakupai lived beside a freshwater lagoon. He had married two sisters, Kuraruna and Jaknia. Jirakupai is credited with being an expert spear maker, of both the large many barbed male *spears*, which have a row of barbs on one side, and the smaller female spears with their double row of barbs. He had just finished making a number of these spears when a raiding party from *Melville Island* rushed into his camp and speared him in the back many times. In retaliation, he pulled the spears out and cast them back at his attackers, then he

retreated by diving into the water. To avoid capture his wives
turned themselves into birds, Kuraruna becoming the night-heron
and Jaknia the brown heron which frequents the mangrove
swamps.

The next morning, his enemies saw Jirakupai floating on the
water, no longer a man but a crocodile. The spear wounds in his
back had grown into a spinal crest, his mouth had grown into a
long snout and his bundle of spears had been transformed into his
tail, on the extreme end of which was his male spear with barbs
along only one side.

See also *Kulama ceremonies*.

Jiritja See *Yiritja*.

Jitta Jitta See *Willy Wagtail*.

Jugambal See *Bundjalung nation*.

Jugumbir See *Bundjalung nation*.

Jukulpa See *Winbaraku*.

Julama See *Thomas, Rover*.

Jungai See *Bandjalung nation*.

Jurumu the wedge-tailed eagle See *Kulama ceremonies;
Mundungkala*.

Juwuku See *Universe*.

K

Kulama yam

Kabi people See *Cherbourg Aboriginal settlement*.

Kaboka the thrush See *Floods*.

Kadigal See *Eora tribe*.

Kadimakara See *Extinct giant marsupials*.

Kakadu National Park Kakadu National Park in the Northern Territory includes the area watered by the East Alligator river system. The traditional owners, the Bunitj *community* of the larger Gagudju people, have leased this area to the Australian government as a national park. The park contains hundreds of sacred sites and has the best rock art I have seen in Australia.

See also *Bark paintings; Darwin; Neidjie, Bill; Oobarr; Rock paintings; Warramurrungundji*.

Kalkadoon people The Kalkadoon people of Queensland were a strong tribe who waged a long campaign against the invaders of their land. A battle was fought in 1884 in which massed warriors stormed a well-fortified position. They continued the attack, even though suffering heavy casualties, but were eventually defeated.

Kameragal See *Eora tribe*.

Karatgurk See *Crow*.

Karluk See *Hydra*.

Karora See *Bandicoot ancestor*.

Katatjuta (or the Olgas) Some 50 kilometres west of *Uluru*, Ayer's Rock, and made up of more than 50 domes of rock, Katatjuta rises some 600 metres above the plains. It is said to be a sacred female place, but its custodians have refused to divulge the mythology, and what has been already published may or may not be true.

Men should not venture into Katatjuta, so I have not been there, but from a distance, it appeared to me like the body of a giant female, lying eroded from sunlight and wind since the *Dreaming* time. Katatjuta has been translated as 'The Place of Many Heads' and a number of Dreaming ancestors are said to be associated with the place. Chief among these, and symbolized by the largest monolith, is the serpent Wanambi, who lives in one of the *waterholes* on top of the tor during the wet season, but during the dry season makes his way to one of the gorges and enters the rock. Thus at least part of the site is sacred to the *rainbow snake* and it is forbidden to light *fires* in the area or drink at the waterhole, lest he become angry and rise to attack.

Many parts of the Katatjuta refer to women, such as the caves on the southern side of Walpa Gorge, which is about 490 metres high. It has been reported that these caves were once piles of corkwood tree blossums collected by the corkwood sisters in the Tjukurrpa or *Dreamtime*. On the eastern side are the camps of the mice women and the curlew man, whose myth formed the basis of a fertility ceremony, details of which are not known.

One highly spectacular pillar of rock is the transformed body of Malu the kangaroo man dying in the arms of his sister Mulumura, a lizard woman. He was killed at this place by a pack of *dogs* after his long journey from the west. His wound is an erosion in the rock and his intestines, which spill out, appear as a rock mound at the base of the pillar.

Other stories relate the tale of the *Pungalunga men* and the ancestral deity, Yuendum, who gave humankind plant foods. All in all Kutatjata appears to be a fertility place of great energy and thus sacred to women.

Katherine Gorge See *Kulunbar*.

Kimberley The Kimberley region of Western Australia is the home country of a number of *Aboriginal* communities, including the Worora, the *Ngarinjin*, the Bunuba and the Wunambul. In the old days these communities only formed at certain times and usually lived in small family groups, sometimes called clans, on their own estates. They were united in a kinship grid and common culture, and came together for festivals and ceremonies. With the coming of the British invaders, the Worora, Ngarinjin and Wunambul peoples were collected together into the Mowanjum settlement just outside Derby.

These shared the same religious belief system, and although their ancestors had given them separate *languages*, they spoke all three, as they met frequently for intertribal ceremonies. They were divided by the ancestral Nightjar men into moieties, or halves, but apparently without subsections or sections, as found in other tribes. Wodoi and Djingun, the moiety deities, decreed in the *Dreamtime* that Wodoi can marry Djingun and Djingun can marry Wodoi. Thus, although there is often rivalry between the two moieties, marriage must always be with a person from the other moiety, so reciprocal relationships are formed which make them interdependent.

See also *Bunuba people; Community; Djamar; Djanggawul and his two sisters myth; Dogs; Eaglehawk and Crow; Giant dogs; Great flood; Mowaljarlal, David; Noonkanbah; Palga; Rainbow snake; Thomas, Rover; Two Men myth; Utemorrah, Daisy; Walmajarri people; Yamadji*.

Kin groups (or skin groups, flesh groups) Many *Aboriginal* communities were divided by the ancestors into what are called sections or subsections, or kin or skin or flesh groups, in that those belonging to the same section are said to have the same flesh, owing to their coming from a common ancestor. By knowing the skin or flesh name of a person, one can know her or his relationship to every other person within the *community*—community rather than tribe, as these skin or flesh group classifications cross over any localized tribal boundaries.

For example in the Walmatjarri there are eight sections or groups divided by gender. These are: (1) Nangala (f), Jangala (m); (2) Nanyjili (f), Jungkurra (m); (3) Nyapurru (f), Jupurru (m); (4) Nyapana (f), Jawanti (m); (5) Nyapajarri (f), Japalyi (m); (6) Nakarra (f), Jakarra (m); (7) Nangkarti (f), Jangkarti (m); (8) Nampiyirnti (f), Jampiyirnti (m). These groups determine marriage partners and on no account should a relationship occur within one's section. This is considered incest and has been banned by the ancestors. Thus a nangala woman should marry a jungkurra man; a nanyjili woman a jangala man; a nyapurru woman a jawanti man; a nyapana woman a jupurru man; a nyappajarri woman a jakarra man; a nakarra woman a japalyi man; a nangkarti woman a jampiyirnti man; and a nampiyirnti woman a jangkarti man. In this case, there is matrilineal descent, the choice of skin group depends on the mother's group and the groups are so arranged that over the generations a complete circle is made with successive generations passing through the groups. In the case of patrilinear descent, that is, through the father, the father's group would determine the offspring's skin, but this is unusual.

Kinship and skin groups are very important in Aboriginal society and it must be remembered that even in Aboriginal mythology the different ancestors are related to each other according to the kinship or skin patterns and thus part of the mesh of family relationships which unites *Aborigines* across Australia.

See also *Community; Kinship; Tribes.*

King Brown Snake See *Oobarr*.

Kinship Kinship forms the basis of all ordering of *Aboriginal* societies. It may be biologic or what is called 'classificatory'. Thus the Aboriginal population as a whole may be said to have been organized across Australia in many families which entered into relationships with each other to form a family or kinship grid all across Australia. There were variations in the classifications, but these could be worked out when the need arose.

See also *Community; Kin groups; Tribes.*

Koala The koala is sometimes called the koala bear. It is a bearlike marsupial which lives in trees and eats only the leaves of certain eucalyptus trees. In Victoria the koala was considered to be a friend and gave helpful advice.

There are a number of *Koori* myths about the koala. One is about the orphan boy Koob-borr, who once during a drought was refused any water by the rest of his people. When he was left alone in his village, he filled all the containers of water from the last flowing creek and hid them up a tree. When the people returned he refused to give them any water and knocked down anyone who tried to climb the tree. Finally, two men caught him and dragged him to the ground. He turned into a koala and quickly ran up another tree for safety. The men cut down the other tree and water flowed back into the creek. From that time koalas became food for the people, but they were not allowed to strip koalas of their skins or use koala fur in ceremonies, because if they did the koala would capture the water again.

See also *Yugumbir people*.

Kolet the dove See *Childbirth*.

Kongkong the fishhawk See *Spears*.

Koob-borr See *Koala*.

Kookaburra See *Emu; Taboo countries*.

Koopoo See *Kulunbar*.

Koori The Koori people live in the states of Victoria, Tasmania and the southern parts of New South Wales. In Victoria, in the old days they were spread across the land in 38 distinct groups, each with their own language. These groups were collected together into five nations. These were the Kulin, the Mara, the Wotjobaluk, the Kurnai and the Ya-itma-thang. Other *tribes* extended along the *Murray river*. With the arrival of the European settlers and large-scale massacres, together with the dispossession of their lands, the remnants of the 38 groups were collected into a number of missions without regard to nation, language or culture. Over time the collectivized people called themselves Koori, which means 'people', but the 38 groups still have a nominal existence and revitalization movements keep parts of the old culture alive, though much has been irretrievably lost.

See also *Aboriginal and Aborigine; Aldebaran; Altair; Antares; Arcturus; Aurora Australis; Berak, William; Bootes; Bull-roarer; Bunjil; Canis Major; Canopus; Centaurus; Coma Berenices; Community; Cooper, William; Corroboree; Cosmography; Crow; Delphinus; Dorabauk; Dreaming tree of life; Eaglehawk and Crow; Emu; Eora tribe; Fomalhaut; Frog; Galaxy; Gondwanaland; Ground carvings and sculptures; Herbal medicines; Hydra; Koala; Magellan Clouds; Marmoo; Mundjauin; Murray river; New moon; Oyster Cove; Rigel; Shamans; Sirius; Southern Cross; Sun; Taboo countries; Tasmania; Trickster character; Trugerninni; White Lady; Wirnum; Yarra river and Port Phillip.*

Kulama ceremonies The kulama ceremonies of *Melville Island* are initiation rituals into a religious cult which is open to both men and women. The corpus of rituals centres around the monsoon and *yams*. Its name, kulama, comes from the name of a poisonous yam which holds central place in the ceremony. The yams, when prepared and cooked in a special manner, are considered to give strength, vitality and good health.

The ceremonies date back to the *Dreamtime*, or *palaneri* (creation) time, when all the animals and birds were men and women. Purutjikini, a boobook owl man and his wife, Pintoma, a barn owl woman performed the first Kulama ceremony on Bathurst Island. They invited Jirakati, later the white-headed sea eagle, and Tupatupini, the small owl, to be present, planning to make them the first initiates. Many other people assisted in the ceremony: the Ningauis, a small spirit people who live in mangrove swamps; Inwati, Mauwini and Tararalili, three groups of *honey* people; *Jirakupai* the salt water crocodile, Narina the *black* cockatoo, and Jurumu the wedge-tailed eagle. A number of ancestral people from Melville Island refused to attend.

The second Kulama ceremony was organized by the Ningauis spirit people on the same island. On its completion they decreed that the form of the ceremony, with its proceedings and initiation rituals, should always be the same.

See also *Initiation process*.

Kulin See *Antares; Balayang; Bunjil; Centaurus; Death; Koori; Taboo countries*.

Kulkunbulla See *Orion*.

Kulunbar (Katherine Gorge) is in Jawoyn country in the Northern Territory and is an important nexus of *Dreaming tracks* and *song lines*. One of the most important ancestors is Koopoo the red plains kangaroo, who after a number of adventures descended into a deep waterhole and became a *rainbow snake*. It is said that the gorge was made by him.

The gorge is very spectacular with the river winding between towering sandstone walls for 12 kilometres. To the south are the sacred hot springs of Mataranka and to the north are the Douglas hot springs.

Kumpinulu See *Sun*.

Kunapipi See *Gunabibi*.

Kuniya See *Uluru*.

Kunnawarra See *Balayang*.

Kungkarangkalpa See *Pleiades*.

Kuraruna See *Jirakupai*.

Kuringgai See *Eora tribe*.

Kuringgai Chase National Park Kuringgai Chase National Park is 30 kilometres north of Sydney and owned by the Kuringgai *Aboriginal community*. It is an area rich in rock art: carvings of whales, sharks and fish, kangaroos and depictions of their great ancestor *Biame*.
See also *Rock paintings*.

Kurinpi women See *Women ancestral beings*.

Kurnai See *All-Fathers; Aurora Australis; Frog; Koori; Mundjauin; Shamans*.

Kurok-goru See *Crow*.

Kurukadi See *Two Men myth*.

Kurung people See *Yarra river and Port Phillip*.

Kururuk See *Balayang*.

Kutji spirits
The kutji spirits usually dwell in the shade of bushes and in deep
holes and show themselves in various forms, such as a *black crow*,
eagle, owl, kangaroo or *emu*. Birds possessed by the kutji differ
from ordinary birds or animals by circling around a person's head
or behaving in an odd manner. In warm weather the kutji may be
a black rain-cloud, or present in a dust-storm, thunder or in a dis-
tant mirage.

These spirits cause sickness, disease, distress and *death*. Only
the shaman can control them. In fact *shamans* receive their power
from them and are in direct communication with them. It is this
direct relationship which gives the shaman his or her healing and
magical arts.

Kwinkan See *Quinkin*.

Kwinkin See *Quinkin*.

Kyowee See *Sun*.

L

Lightning brother

Labumore (Elsie Roughsey) (1923—) Labumore is a member of the Lardil people of Goonana (*Mornington Island*) in the gulf of Carpentaria. She has been actively engaged in revitalizing her culture on the island and has had her autobiography published: *An Aboriginal Mother Tells of the Old and the New* (1984).

Laindjung See *Barama and Laindjung myths*.

Languages It is not known how many languages were spoken in Australia before the invasion of the Europeans. A figure of 250 is sometimes given, but often language shades into dialect and people often prefer their tongue to be known as language rather than dialect. Thus the languages of the *Western Desert*, spoken over a million square kilometres, can be shown to be related to one another and form a huge network of different dialects, though each *community* wishes its dialect to be known as a language.

The survival of many languages is uncertain, owing to the

predominance of English, but there are periodic attempts at language revitalization, as amongst my people, the *Nyungar*, which keep at least aspects of the language alive. In the old days many *Aborigines* were bi- or multi-lingual, owing to the prevalence of cultural attributes, such as marriage and ceremony, which crossed over so-called language barriers.

Lardil people See *Giant dogs; Labumore; Mornington Island; Roughsey, Dick*.

Laura Laura in northern Queensland is a site rich in *Aboriginal* rock art. The art features animals, birds, spirit beings, *shamans* and people. The rock galleries have a number of sorcery figures which the desperate defenders drew and sought to use as magical weapons in their resistance against the invaders.

In the myths of the area, stories are told of a *black* bird with a long neck which steals the bones of the dead. On some of the images of the invaders, recognizable by their rifles and revolvers, this bird is standing, pecking into their flesh.

Laura is also the home of the spirit beings called *Quinkin*. Each year an important *dance* festival is held there.

See also *Cape York peninsula; Rock paintings*.

Lightning Lightning, according to the Wardaman people of the Northern Territory, is caused by two brothers who carried hammers and struck them to cause the thunder and lightning. They descended into the *earth* at *Ingelaladd*.

See also *Bolung; Gunabibi ceremonies; Idumdum; Monsoon; Rain-making; Taipan; Trickster character; Universe; Wandjina; Warramurrungundji; Yulunggul*.

Lightning Brothers See *Lightning*.

Liru people See *Uluru*.

Lo-an See *Taboo countries*.

Lo-an-tuka See *Taboo countries*.

Looma the blue tongue lizard woman See *Pea Hill*.

Luma Luma the giant Luma Luma the giant gave the designs painted on the chests of the Gunwinggu people of *Arnhem Land* during ceremonies. These ochre designs are many fine criss-crossed lines forming intricate patterns. Each segment of design represents an area of the man's ancestral country.

Luma Luma is a cultural hero who is said to have come from over the sea from the direction of Indonesia. He was attacked by the tribesmen as a stranger, but taught the people paintings and *dances* before returning whence he had come.

See also *Bark paintings; Sleeping giant.*

Lumbiella See *Dogs.*

M

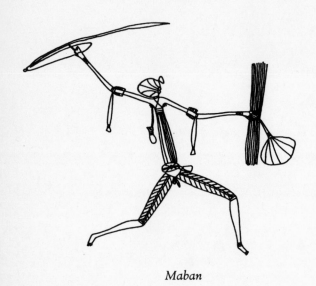

Maban

Maban See *Shamans*.

Madkandyi the Terrible Whirlwind The myth of Madkandyi the Terrible Whirlwind is narrated by the *elders* of the *Adnyamathanha people*. It is said that once a huge whirlwind arose in Western Australia and rushed east towards New South Wales. The whirlwind came rushing towards the *Flinders Range*, hit them and pivoted around them in a clockwise direction and when it got to the other side, it stopped. This is why all the sand dunes are seen in ridges pointing towards the range.

Mafi-Williams, Lorraine See *Byron Bay*.

Magellan Clouds The Lesser and Greater Magellan Clouds were believed by the Wotjobaluk and Mara *Koori* peoples to represent the female and male native companion ancestors.

Magic cord See *Shamans; Spirit snake*.

Mai Korpi See *Mangrove woman*.

Malagi See *Djang*.

Malbaru See *Bindirri, Yirri*.

Malu the kangaroo man See *Katatjuta*.

Maludaianiniu See *Universe*.

Malumba See *Bralgu*.

Mamoon See *Bundjalung nation*.

Mamu-boijunda the barking spider See *Walbiri creation myth; Winbaraku*.

Mana boming See *Trade*.

Manangananga cave See *Arrernte people*.

Mandya the euro See *Flinders Range*.

Mangalamarra, George See *Palga*.

Mangrove woman The myth of the mangrove woman is narrated by the *elders* of the *Wik Munggan* people.
   Mai Korpi the mangrove woman was the ancestor who taught
women the way of preparing the edible mangrove seed. It is said
that once in the *Dreamtime*, Wolkolan, who later became the bony
bream fish, went to see his sisters. He was tired when he got there
and asked his sisters to bring him food, but his elder sister had
been making mangrove flour and said that she was tired too.
Wolkolan threatened her and she picked up her digging stick and
hit him on the shoulder. In return, Wolkolan speared her in the
head and the spear stayed in. His sister fled and went to a flat
place and into the *earth* there. It became her *auwa*, or *djang* place.

The spear was still sticking out from her head, just as the mangrove pod sticks out from its petals. Now women gather mangrove pods and make flour there, just as she did.

Mantya the death-adder See *Taipan*.

Mara people See *Hydra; Koori; Magellan Clouds; Sirius*.

Mara the sugar ant See *Two Brothers*.

Maralga See *Warmalana*.

Marindi the giant dog See *Parachilna; Red ochre*.

Marmoo To the *Koori* people, Marmoo was the evil spirit, in opposition to *Biame*. He was jealous of Biame's and *Yhi*'s creation and countered this with the creation of insects. Biame came together with Nungeena, the spirit of the waterfalls, to stop Marmoo's plague of insects by creating birds. Nungeena fashioned a pattern of flowers into which Biame breathed life. It became a lyre bird, the most beautiful of birds, and began scratching for insects. Biame created more birds and they destroyed the insects or kept them under control. Biame gave them their voices as a reward for their services.

Marnbi the bronze-winged pigeon Marnbi the bronze-winged pigeon is associated with gold (his blood) and white quartz (his feathers). The Adnyamathanha *elders* narrate the myth which connects him to these minerals and their mines.

Once a man made a net to catch bronze-winged pigeons. A flock of them came along and he flung the net over them. He struck at them with his club, but one of them, Marnbi, somehow managed to escape. He rose into the air and fled, dropping feathers and specks of blood as he went. At places where he rested, he left more blood and feathers, and these became a source of gold and quartz. He flew into New South Wales and went north to Mount Isa where the big mine is still operating.

See also *Opals; Quartz crystal*.

Marnbil See *Mornington Island*.

Marpean-kurrk See *Arcturus; Bootes*.

Marriage rules See *Kin groups*.

Mars Among the *Murray river* people, Mars was Bilyarra, the eaglehawk ancestor.

Marwai the master painter The *Dreaming* ancestor Marwai the master painter is believed to have been the keeper and distributor of designs in western *Arnhem Land*. He travelled about the country, carrying chips of ochre colours in a dilly bag hanging from his neck. As he travelled, he rested at various caves and rock shelters, and then he took out his colours, ground them to a fine powder and painted paintings on the walls of caves and shelters which may still be seen today.

Marwai was also a teacher. He taught the people he met on his travels how to paint his designs. The great Gunwinggu painter *Yirawala*, who has been called the Picasso of Australia, gained his skills from Marwai and painted several portraits of the great master painter.

See also *Rock paintings*.

Master Moon See *Shamans*.

Matchwood tree The matchwood tree (*Erythroxylum ellipticum*) is the *Dreaming tree of life* and *death* for the *tribes* of *Cape York peninsula*. When a person dies it is believed that the soul climbs this tree to the *sky world*. The body is taken to the clan burial ground and a small matchwood tree is uprooted and the top cut off to leave a metre high stump which is stuck upside-down on the grave.

The matchwood has a shallow, flat root system with a main taproot. The taproot is oriented towards the west, where the entrance to the sky world is said to be. After the third day the soul ascends from the nostrils of the dead person and passes through the trunk to the flatroot system, which forms a platform. It is very confused and sits there until it sees the taproot pointing west, whereupon it flies off in that direction to the entrance to the sky world. The entrance to the sky world is in the shape of an inverted y-shaped tree trunk which can be slammed down to prevent spirits from entering. It is guarded by an ancestral deity whose name is secret. The guardian spirit makes the soul laugh so that he can check to see if it has passed through initiation, in which a front tooth is removed. The body of the soul is also checked for sacred signs. If all is well, the soul is allowed to pass through the portal.

When a baby is born the mother buries the afterbirth beneath the matchwood tree and as soon as the child is able it is encouraged to climb it.

See also *Tree between Heaven and Earth*.

Mauwini See *Kulama ceremonies*.

Mbu the ghost Mbu the ghost is the patron of funeral rites among the Ndraangit people of *Cape York peninsula*. He became the patron as he was the first for whom rites were held.

Tyit the fish hawk, Mbu's brother, introduced the rites after he and Mbu had fought over a turtle they had speared and Mbu had been killed in the fight. Tyit covered him with bark, cut open his side and took out his intestines and liver. He tied the body to a long pole, put it across forked sticks and dried it over a *fire*. Then he covered the dried out body with bark and carried it back to their parents. They held a funeral service for Mbu to send him on his way and sang him to his place of rest so that he would not come back to haunt them.

See also *Death*.

Meendie giant snake See *Bunyip*.

Mekigar See *Shamans*.

Melatji Law Dogs See *Dogs; Winbaraku*.

Melbourne The area on which the city of Melbourne now stands was once an important meeting-place for the three *tribes* of the surrounding countryside: the Wurundjeri, the Bunurong and the Watharung. Port Phillip Bay, on which the city stands, is said to have been created by *Bunjil* the eaglehawk ancestor (see *Yarra river and Port Phillip*).

See also *Berak, William; Crow*.

Melville Island Melville Island, off the coast of northern Australia, is the home of the *Tiwi people*. The Tiwis ascribe the creation of the island to an old blind woman, *Mudungkala*, who crawled over the then bare land and made the island, separating it from the mainland. As her final act, she decreed that the bare land should be clothed in vegetation and inhabited by creatures. She then crawled southwards and disappeared, leaving behind her children, two girls and a boy, who became the ancestors of the Tiwi.

See also *Bark paintings; Curlews; Cyclops; Jirakupai; Kulama ceremonies; Mopaditis; Pukamani funeral ceremonies; Spirit children; Sun; Tokumbimi Tokumbimi; Tree between Heaven and Earth.*

Menstrual blood Menstrual blood, in all *Aboriginal* communities and clans, was a source of *djang*, power and magic. When a woman was menstruating she had to stay apart from the main camp.

Amongst the *Wik Munggan* people, menstrual blood was associated with the *rainbow snake*, the magic shaman serpent, *Taipan*. There is a woman's myth or *Dreaming* story from this area showing the connection between Taipan and women's fertility, blood and milk.

Yuwam, the *black* snake with red under its belly, ran away with Ita the swamp-fish man, who was in the category of 'son' to her husband, Tintauwa, the black water snake, and thus they were committing incest. Taipan, as her mother's brother and upholder of the law, followed to punish this 'wrong way' relationship. He caught up with her and created a bog or swamp around her so that she could not escape, although Ita managed to run away.

Yuwam had daughters who were swimming in a lagoon nearby. They were completely hairless and had no breasts or organs, or periods. Taipan went to them and the whole area turned red. The frightened girls tried to hide, rubbing mud over their heads, their chests and between their legs. They dove under the water and later emerged to find that they had long hair on their heads, tufts under their arms and pubic hair. They also had breasts.

Yuwam, the mother, tried to rise from beneath the bog she had been trapped in, but could not. She kept sinking deeper and deeper. Taipan said to her, 'My girl, my sister's daughter, you have received this punishment from your mother's *earth*.' He smoothed a spot and pulled out some grass and said, 'Some blood, I have brought you, woman. The rest I will carry windward and spill there at my sacred place.' He made a hole in the ground for the blood he gave to the woman and put it there for her. This became 'forbidden' ground. It was at the foot of a bloodwood tree—the menstrual blood. Taipan said that Yuwam would become a snake with a red belly and so she did.

He also put some milk at the foot of a milkwood tree and said, 'When women are grown up, milk shall come to them all from this milkwood tree. People everywhere will come to this place, to this

tree, for babies. You will give a girl baby to the women who come
here. Girl babies will come from this fertility place of yours,
Yuwam.' And Yuwam sank beneath the surface and the place is
sacred to her and is a fertility site for women who want girl babies.

See also *Conception beliefs; Gender roles; Sun*.

Midgegooroo See *Yagan*.

Milky Way The Milky Way is considered by some *Aboriginal* communities to be a river called Milnguya. In the *Dreamtime*, *Crow*
and Cat built a fishtrap from stone. It was the very first fishtrap
and the model for all other fishtraps. Unfortunately, Crow and
Cat caught Balin the barramundi in it and he was eaten by the
members of their *community*. Crow and Cat were aghast when
they came to the beach and discovered this. Wahn, Crow, was
related to Balin the barramundi and gave him a fitting burial.
Placing his bones in a hollow tree, Crow and Cat took the *hollow
log coffin* up into the sky and placed it beside the river, Milnguya,
the Milky Way. Then they decided to stay up there too. So now
when we look up into the sky, up at the Milky Way, we see stars
that are campfires of Crow and Cat. Some of the other stars are
the spots found on the body of Native Cat and some are the
hollow log coffin, while the dark patches are the outspread wings
of Crow.

See also *Dreaming tree of life; Inma boards; Universe*.

Millstream pools Millstream in the Pilbara is an important series
of sacred sites which were made in the *Dreaming* by the *Rainbow
snake*. It is said that in the Dreaming two young men caught and
ate a ring-necked parrot which was taboo to them. The serpent
smelt it cooking and came from the sea to punish them. As it
dragged itself along, it made the Fortesque river coming from the
north. It cut the river in half by making *waterholes* at Gregory
Gorge. It went underground and when it emerged at different
places, it made waterpools. It descended on the boys in the shape
of a whirlwind and swallowed them up. The people cried and
protested and the giant snake became angry and drowned them in
a sudden downpour of water.

Milnguya See *Milky Way*.

Mimi spirits The mimi spirit people are said to be thin stick-like
spirits who inhabit the rock crevasses and bush of *Arnhem Land*

and are similar to the *Quinkin* found in northern Queensland. They are said to be very artistic as well as fine hunters and they expressed themselves by painting their portraits on the rocks. These are painted almost exclusively in *red ochre* and range from pale red to darkest brown. They depict the mimi hunting, spearing kangaroos, running and dancing. They are among the finest and most elegant of *rock paintings* found in Australia.

See also *Bark paintings*.

Min Kakalang See *Spears*.

Min Kena See *Crocodiles*.

Minjelungin See *Wagyal*.

Minjungbal See *Bundjalung nation*.

Miralaidj See *Djanggawul and his two sisters myth*.

Mirdinan See *Animal behaviour; Trickster character*.

Mirrabooka See *Southern Cross*.

Mirritji, Jack See *Duwa moiety*.

Mityan the moon Mityan the *moon* was a native cat who fell in love with one of the wives of Unurgunite, the small star between the large ones of *Canis Major*. In the ensuring fight, he was driven away to wander ever since through the heavens.

Moiety ancestor Many *Aboriginal* communities are divided into two halves or 'moieties', which are often named after a *Dreaming* ancestral spirit who is considered the primordial ancestor of the groups or clans in the moiety, each of which also has its own Dreaming ancestry, so sometimes the moeity ancestor is considered the father and the clan ancestors his sons.

See also *Eaglehawk and Crow*.

Moinee See *Tasmanian creation myth*.

Moipaka The moipaka *bull-roarer* series of the Wik Kalkan symbolize the various phases through which men and women pass, in
relationship to either gender, through puberty, marriage to
parenthood. Each phase is represented by an ancestral being
who gives not only the bull-roarer, but also the *djang* place where
it is energized.

A moipaka painted with white spots on a red background represents a young married woman and is used in illicit relationships:
it is swung outside the camp by a married man in order to attract
a young married woman. The woman is attracted by the sound,
but when she is near the swinger quickly hides the bull-roarer, as
otherwise it would lose its effect. This moipaka was first made and
used by the two cockatoo brothers.

Another moipaka, red with white stripes, symbolizes a married
woman who has borne a child. This mother moipaka is swung to
celebrate the birth of the first child.

There is also a male moipaka which, when swung with the
female one, symbolizes the institution of marriage and married
life.

Moiya and pakapaka Moiya and pakapaka are two *bull-roarer*s
which belong to the *Wik Munggan* people and there are two
others, *moipaka* (male and female) which belong to the allied
Wik Kalkan.

The moiya symbolizes a young girl just entering puberty. It is a
small, plain piece of wood and is swung by young initiates at the
end of the first part of the man-making ceremonies.

The pakapaka symbolizes a fully mature woman. It is a longer
and broader tongue-shaped piece of wood, painted red and white
and fastened to a string. It is swung at the end of the initiation
ceremony.

The myth about these bull-roarers concerns two initiates of the
first man-making ceremonies, who at the end of the ceremonies
break taboos by eating flying fox and speaking to and sharing their
food with girls. As a punishment the two initiates are carried off
by the flying fox and the girls are swept by a tide downriver onto
a rock where two of them find a moiya and swing it as they sing,
'What is this we are swinging into the clouds, which is forbidden?
What is this we two are swinging?' Then they place it in the crack
of a bloodwood tree with the remark, 'It belongs to us women, we
found it. It belongs to us, but let it be. Leave it for the men, they'll
always use it.' They then descend into their *auwa*, or *djang* place.

The myth underlies the initiation ceremonies of the Wik
Munggan and symbolizes the awakening interest in the other sex
at puberty and how it should be controlled.

See also *Initiation process*.

Molonga ceremonies The Molonga ceremonies were similar to the Ghost Dance of the Native Americans and arose in response to the invasion of Australia. The central figure was Molonga, a supernatural revenge demon, and it is said that at the end of the ceremonies the demon swallowed up all Europeans.

The ceremonies first came to notice in 1897, when they were being performed on the northern Georgina river in Queensland. From there they spread over the next 25 years to Alice Springs, Lake Eyre and the southern coastline of the Nullabor Plain. It is unfortunate that they are no longer performed today, for from all accounts they were most dramatic and different from other *Aboriginal* ceremonies.

Monsoon (Barra) The north-west monsoon, Barra, is surrounded and explained by a whole circle of myths enacted out in ceremonies and songs. It is connected to the *rainbow snake Warramurrungundji* and the *Lightning* Brothers.

See also *Bolung; Seasons; Universe; Warramurrungundji; Wawilak sisters*.

Moon The moon is always masculine and there are many stories explaining his origin. Amongst some *Aboriginal* groups, the rays of the moon were felt to be harmful to a person. If a man looked at the moon too long, he would fall into a trance.

See also *Death; Eclipse of the moon; First woman; Mityan the moon; New moon; Universe*.

Mopaditis The mopaditis are the spirits of the dead on *Melville Island*, according to the *Tiwi people* living there. They live in the various totemic or *djang* places on Melville and Bathurst Islands and are similar to human beings, except that their bodies no longer have substance. They are invisible by day, but appear white at night and can walk on the surface of water. They live in their spirit lands much in the manner of human beings.

If a small child dies, its mopaditi stays in the immediate neighbourhood, sleeping with the mother until morning, then leaving when it is daylight. After some months, this spirit child, called a *buda-buda*, re-enters the body of its previous mother through her vagina and begins life again.

When an older person dies, his or her mopaditi stays around the grave, mourning its relatives, for three days, then after this it sets off to the locality where it was born, which in the old days would have been its totemic or *djang* site. As it travels, flocks of *black* cockatoos fly screeching overhead to tell the spirits at its birth-place that it is coming to them. It stays there with them until the funeral services begin, then they all go to watch the living perform the *dances* and ceremonies. At night, when the living mourners have gone to sleep, the spirits enter the ceremonial ground to conduct the same ceremonies. At the conclusion of the final *puka-mani*, the mopaditi returns to its birthplace, where it is treated as a youth and must undergo initiation again.

Sometimes the mopaditis contact the living and when this hap-pens a human being's hair will stand on end and his skin go clammy. Sometimes the haunted person is paralysed, goes into a fit and foams at the mouth. This is called 'mopaditi sickness' and can be cured by heating wads of paperbark and pressing them against the sides of the person's face or over the ears until the muscles relax.

Mopoke See *Owl*.

Morning Star Bornumbirr, the Morning Star, is represented in *Arnhem Land* ceremonies by an ornately decorated pole. This pole is tightly bound with string, except for the very top and bottom sections. Sacred symbols in *red ochre* or *white ochre* are painted over the top of the string and the various feathers on the pole are bound into it. The very top of the pole is painted white and the 'eye' of Morning Star is inserted into it. The rest of the pole is painted with symbols of the different *wangarr* or spirit beings.

When a person dies, the spirit is taken across the sea in a spirit canoe which follows the trail of light falling from Bornumbirr. The spirit goes to Baralku (*Bralgu*), an island beyond the sunrise, where it is greeted by the spirits of those who have gone before. The Morning Star is thus a symbol of eternity and the continuance of life after *death*.

The *Adnyamathanha people* see the Morning Star, Warta Vurdli, 'big star', as being male and connect it to their man-making rites. Warta Vurdli had two sons. He made a law which forbade boys who had not been made men to eat kangaroo meat. His two sons took no notice of this law, however, and they and their friends ate kangaroo flesh. Moreover, when they hunted, they brought back to the *elders* only small kangaroos. Warta Vurdli decided to punish the boys, although they were his sons. He took a small kangaroo the boys had left for him and cut it in half. He blew on both halves and created two groups of kangaroos, blue and red, and let them

go. He called his sons to show them the kangaroos. The two boys
and their friends rushed off to the hunt. Just as they came upon
the kangaroos, he caused all of them and their throwing sticks to
float up to the sky. While he watched, he twisted the haft of his
spear into the ground, then dropped into the hole in the ground
and became the Morning Star. He did this so that he would not be
near his disobedient sons. To this day, the Morning Star always
rises when the other stars are setting or is setting when his sons
and their friends are rising.

See also *Djanggawul and his two sisters myth; First woman; Island
of the Dead; Morning Star song series of Arnhem Land; Rom ceremony
of Arnhem Land.*

Morning Star song series of Arnhem Land The *Morning Star*
song series is a number of sacred songs which are sung in *Arnhem
Land* at important ceremonies such as initiations. An important
song about the Morning Star gives its name to the whole series. A
rough translation is:

Morning Star comes and confronts the dawn, a cluster of
Morning star confronts the dawn, coming from the red ochre
country, Morning Star, Bornumbirr, Morning Star is coming,
true bone, the substance of Bornumbirr, orange and with a
white feathered string bound around her body, around the
Morning Star pole.

Mornington Island (Goonana), off the northern coast of
Australia is the home of the Lardil people. The creative ancestor
of the *Dreamtime* is Marnbil, who made many of the geographical
features of the island. *Labumore* of the Lardil people tells the story
of Marnbil, his wife Gin-Gin and his nephew Dewaliwall. They
came from the west to the island and created trees and rocks, fish
traps, *waterholes* and freshwater streams. They gave names to the
different foods, sea and land, then at their last camp Marnbil
killed Dewaliwall because he made love to his aunt Gin-Gin.
See also *Giant dogs; Gondwanaland; Roughsey, Dick.*

Mother-in-law avoidance In many *Aboriginal* communities, it
was forbidden for the son-in-law to speak to his wife's mother, or
often even to notice her presence.
See *Murray river; Rigel.*

Mount Bingingerra See *Yugumbir people.*

Mount Castle See *Sleeping giant*.

Mount Lindsay See *Jalgumbun*.

Mount Maroon See *Yugumbir people*.

Mount Serle See *Arta-wararlpanha*.

Mount Tabletop Mount Tabletop is in the country of the Yuggera people of Queensland. It is now in the Lockyer district and is an important sacred place, though the ceremonies held there have long stopped. In the 1840s it was the base for a resistance movement against the invaders.

Mount Warning See *Wollumbin*.

Mount Widgee See *Dogs*.

Mount Witheren See *Yugumbir people*.

Mowaljarlai, David (*c.*1928–) David Mowaljarlai is an elder of the Ngarinyin people of the *Kimberley* region of Western Australia. He is a powerful exponent of his culture and his teachings and the life of his people are detailed in the book *Yorro*.
   See also *Gondwanaland; Utemorrah, Daisy; Wullunggnari; Waterholes*.

Mparntwe See *Arremte landscape of Alice Springs*.

Mudati the fork-tailed kite See *Mudungkala*.

Mudu See *Eagle*.

Mudungkala was seen as the All-Mother ancestor of the *Tiwi people* of *Melville Island* and other islands off the coast of northern Australia. She made the islands, coated them in vegetation, then crawled off, leaving her two daughters, Wuriupranala and Murupiangkala, with their brother Purukupali.
   Purukupali visited one of the homes of the *spirit children*, the

Pitipituis, and brought some back and gave them to his sisters so that they might have children. Murupiangkala had one daughter, Tukumbuna, who married Wilindu. Tukumbuna had two daughters, Wilunduela and Numanirakala and a son, Tukimbini. Tukimbini's wife, Waia, gave birth to a daughter, Bima, who became the wife of Purukupali. It was the *death* of their son, Djinini, which brought the *Dreamtime* to an end. Wuriupranala had one son, Wuriuprinili.

In those times there was neither light nor heat and the descendants of old Mudungkala had to grope around in the darkness for their food and, when they found it, eat it raw. It was then that Jurumu (later the wedge-tailed eagle) and Mudati (the fork-tailed kite) discovered *fire* and Purukupali realized that it was good. Now they had fire to dispel the darkness, to keep them warm and to cook their food. Purukupali gave a torch of bark to his sister Wuriupranala and told her that it was her duty to always keep it alight (see also *Sun*).

With the coming of light, the descendants of Mudungkala spread over the island and camped at places which would after the end of the Dreamtime become their *djang* centres. While many of the people of the Dreamtime were spreading over the island, the original family and their descendants established themselves on south-eastern Melville Island at Impanali.

Purukupali was strongly attached to his son, Djinini, and when his wife, Bima, went out food gathering, she would take him with her, bringing him back to Purukupali at the end of the day, together with the food she had collected. But at Impanali there also lived an unmarried man, Japara, who used to persuade Bima to leave her child asleep under the shade of a tree and go off into the forest with him. One hot day, Bima went off with Japara and stayed away too long. The shade moved and when she returned she found Djinini lying dead from the hot *sun*. When Purukupali heard of the death of his son, his grief and anger knew no bounds. He struck his wife a blow on the head with his throwing stick and hunted her through the forest while cursing the living beings of the world. He said that as his son had died so the whole of creation would die and, once dead, would never come back to life. Japara remonstrated with Purukupali, telling him that he could restore Djinini's life in three days, but instead of being pacified, Purukupali attacked him. Japara defended himself and in the fight both were wounded.

Purukupali picked up the body of his dead son, which Bima had wrapped in a sheet of paperbark, and walked backwards into the sea, calling out as he did so, 'You must all follow me; as I die, so must you die.' The place where he entered the sea became a whirlpool upon which no canoe could live. When Japara saw what had happened, he changed himself into the *moon*.

With the entry of death into the world, the Dreamtime came to an end and the present time began. This myth, which I have given in some detail, is the foundation of the elaborate *Pukamani funeral ceremonies* of the Tiwi.

Mukama the black flying fox See *Flying foxes*.

Mullamulluns See *Shamans*.

Mulumura the lizard woman See *Katatjuta*.

Mulyan the eaglehawk See *Trickster character*.

Mumba See *Two Men myth*.

Mumbulla state forest Mumbulla state forest in south-eastern New South Wales contains the sacred mountains of the Yuin people, Goolaga and Mumbulla.

Mundjauin Mundjauin was a famous shaman of the Kurnai *Koori* people of Victoria. He received his powers from kangaroo spirits in a grand spiritual ceremony. Once he disappeared from camp and was found next morning in a trance with a huge log across his back. He was taken back to the camp where he remained in the trance for some time, during which he sang songs about how he had been taken to the *sky world* and was being given powerful songs and incantations there.

Mungan Ngour See *All-Fathers; Aurora Australis*.

Muralaidj See *Djanggawul and his two sisters myth*.

Murlu the kangaroo See *Bunuba people*.

Murray river The Murray river is Australia's longest river and the *Koori* people have a myth about how it was made. Totyerguil was a mighty hunter and one day in his travels he reached the place where the town of Swan Hill now stands and camped there with his two wives, Gunewarra, the *black* swans, and his two sons. The two boys saw a huge fish basking in the *sun* and told their father. Totyerguil ran to the place and speared the fish, Otjout the murray cod. The spear stuck in his back and the cod rushed to the banks of the waterhole and charged off, making the channel which became the Murray river. Totyerguil followed the channel in a canoe, caught up with the cod again and speared him a second time in the back. The cod rushed off, extending the channel, and Totyerguil followed, spearing him in the back at intervals and at different places along the river. The *spears* he threw may be seen as the spines along the back of the fish. Eventually, near Murray Bridge in South Australia, the cod made a deep waterhole and hid. Later, he escaped into the sky to become the star *Delphinus*.

Totyerguil, having thrown all his spears and lost the fish, landed upon the bank where he set his canoe on end and stuck his paddle upright in the ground. The canoe became a huge gum tree and the paddle a murray pine. It is these species of trees that the descendants of Totyerguil use in making their *canoes* and paddles.

Totyerguil now continued his journey and went to the Grampian mountains, where he was to meet his family. He found them on top of a lofty cliff and called to them to jump down. He caught them all except his mother-in-law, Yerrerdet-kurrk, whom he had to ignore because of the mother-in-law taboo. She was injured and as she recovered she plotted revenge. She saw a huge water snake in a deep waterhole and, seizing the opportunity, spread rotten branches and sticks across the top of the waterhole to hide it. She added leaves and grass to make it look like a bandicoot's nest, then she called the two boys and told them to tell their father. She told them to tell him not to spear the bandicoot, as this would spoil its flesh, but to catch the bandicoot with his feet by standing on it.

Totyerguil, who had been feeling guilty about failing to catch his mother-in-law, did as instructed. He leapt into the centre of the nest and fell through into the water below. The giant serpent, disturbed, became enraged. It rushed at him and he threw his *boomerang* at it but missed. The boomerang swirled up into the sky to become the constellation *Corona Borealis*. The giant snake dragged Totyerguil down into the depths of the pool and he was drowned.

Collenbitjik the bull-ant, who was Totyerguil's maternal uncle, jumped into the pool to retrieve the body. He too might have drowned, for the water had become very muddy, but he felt his way out by his fingers, or antennae, which bull-ants have since that time.

Totyerguil is now the star *Altair* and the two smaller stars on either side of him are his two wives. His mother-in-law has become the star *Rigel* and Collenbitjik's fingers have become the double star at the head of *Capricornus*.

This is a particularly fine *Aboriginal* myth and has all the main features of such a myth, though there is much hidden within it, and only the non-secret version is given here. It does show, however, how *mother-in-law avoidance* came into being and how bull-ants got their antennae, as well as how the Murray river was formed. It also shows how such stories are imprinted on natural phenomena so that the whole universe is a text from which a cul-tured Aboriginal person can read the myth.

Murri Murri The name by which all the *Aboriginal* people of Queensland are known.

Murupiangkala See *Mudungkala*.

Mutton bird (*Puffinus tenuirostris*) The mutton bird, a migratory seabird, has become an emblem of the Tasmanian *Aborigines* and is harvested for food when it comes to breed along the coastline of *Tasmania* and the off-lying islands.

The importance of the mutton birds to the Tasmanian Aborigines is told by Laurie Lowery:

I'll try to explain to some of these people from the mainland how the mutton bird travels from one end of the Earth to the other and how they make it in such a short time. When the mutton birds leave, they leave all together. A week before the season finishes, the old birds leave the holes, you see. The young birds are left to fend for themselves by lightening off so they can get into the air.

In the twelve mile radius off those islands they wait, the old birds wait at sea, and when the young birds make it to sea, they meet up with them and they all go on from there.

What happens is, when they hit the air, when they're in flight, there's so many of them, millions of them, millions, and some birds circle towards the centre and another group forms on the outside. That's how they sleep—the birds in the middle sleep and the air currents from the wings of the birds on the outside keep them in flight; it's just like sleeping on an airbed. When the birds on the outside get tired, they fly into the centre and the birds from the centre go to the outside and it's their turn. That's how they survive.

And it takes them seven days from when they get to the northern part of Japan and Alaska. The only bird that can do that is the mutton bird.

N

Numuwuwari the crocodile ancestor

Nabanunga women See *Winbaraku*.

Namatjira, Albert (1902–59) Albert Namatjira was a famous watercolourist of the *Arrernte people*. He was one of the first indigenous artists to receive recognition outside his own *community*. He was feted throughout Australia and considered to be a symbol of the then Australian government's policy of assimilating all Australian *Aborigines* into the invader way of life (see *Assimilation policy*). Up until 1967, when the Australian Constitution was amended by referendum to include all Aboriginal people as citizens of Australia, indigenous people were wards of the state and had no citizenship rights. These had to be earned by the indigenous person, who had to show that he could live as a British person. Albert was given 'citizenship rights' in 1957, but this 'citizenship' caused a rift between him and his family. He rebelled against his position as an 'honorary white', and decided to stick with his family and people. The stress caused by his choice led to his early *death* in August 1959.

Albert's paintings are of the vibrant landscapes of the Arrernte country of central Australia and he has become the inspiration of the landscape school of Arrernte painters which continues in the tradition, though now utilizing motifs from traditional Arrernte culture. Some of the major artists of this school are Therese Ryder, the masterly Wenten Rubuntja and Gordon Waye.

See also *Hermannsburg Mission*.

Nanga *Nanga* is the collective name for the *Aborigines* of South Australia.

See also *Community; Narroondarie; Uniapon, David*.

Nangala See *Pea Hill*.

Nara The *nara* ceremonies are practised by the *Aboriginal* people of *Arnhem Land*. They were taught by the ancestors of the *Duwa* and *Yiritja* moeities in the *Dreamtime*.

See *Djanggawul mythology and ceremonies; Duwa moeity*.

Narina the black cockatoo See *Kulama ceremonies*.

Narrinyini people See *Narroondarie*.

Narroondarie Narroondarie's myth was narrated by *David Uniapon*, a *Nanga* elder of South Australia.

Narroondarie was a cultural hero who came to the Narrinyini people in South Australia. He was sent by the All-Father *Biame* as his messenger and teacher. He came down from the northern parts of Australia, though New South Wales and Victoria, where he was known as Boonah. He came to rest on two bald hills in South Australia close to the lakes Alexandrina and Albert. He was to wait there until he was called by Biame, but one day he saw two young grass trees women who had been trapped in their tree forms. He released the two girls, fell under their spell and took both of them for his wives. He spoke to them of the laws he had made and stated that there was a fish called Tookerrie which was forbidden to women.

One day he had to go on a journey and left his wives alone. Whilst he was away, they caught the Tookerrie fish and ate it. Realizing that they would be punished for breaking the law, the two fled. Narroondarie returned and found the bones of the fish and his wives gone. He set off in pursuit. He followed the tracks of his wives and came across an old camp and found out that they had eaten more forbidden fish. He continued after them southwards towards the coast.

His two wives meanwhile had reached the coast and looked across to Kangaroo Island, which at that time was still joined to the mainland. It was considered a spirit island and once there they would be free of the law. However, instead of crossing, they dallied collecting *honey* and also because the passage to the island was guarded by the blue crane who would not let anyone across without permission. Now Narroondarie sent a message to the blue crane that he should allow the women to step onto the passageway. Once they were halfway across, Narroondarie chanted the wind song. The wind howled and the sea was lashed into a fury of waves and foam and flooded over the strip of *earth*. The two women struggled to swim back to the mainland, but were overcome and drowned. As a visible sign to all women not to eat forbidden food, their bodies were turned into two rocks which are still known today as the Two Sisters.

The storm subsided and Narroondarie walked across to what was to become Kangaroo Island. On its side was a huge gum tree under whose shade he rested until sunset. He then went to the bottom of the sea to rescue the spirits of his two wives and after doing this flew upwards with them to the *sky world* where he lives with Biame to this day.

National Aboriginal Day National Aboriginal Day is celebrated on the second Friday of July. It is a day of celebration and remembrance of our ancestors, as symbolized by the Tasmanian *Aboriginal* woman *Trugerninni*, who died on the second Friday of July 1876. When she died, her skeleton was placed in the Tasmanian museum and kept on display for many years. It was only after years of struggle that the Aboriginal people of Australia were allowed to lay her to rest in the sea as she had wanted.

National Aboriginal Flag The National Aboriginal Flag was designed by Harold Thomas of the Aranda tribe in 1972. The upper *black* half represents the *Aboriginal* people of Australia; the lower red half represents the colour of the land and the blood which was spilt when our indigenous Australia was invaded by the British. The central yellow circle is the *sun*, the giver of all life.

Native companion bird See *Emu; Magellan Clouds*.

Native tobacco See *Palkalina; Pituri*.

Ndraangit people See *Mbu the ghost; Wik Munggan*.

Neidjie, Bill (1920?–) Bill Neidjie of the Bunitj clan of the Gagudju tribe clan is one of the owners of the land now containing the *Kakadu National Park*. He is an important story-teller, anxious that his culture and myths should continue. His teachings are found in two books, *Kakadu Man* (1985) and *Story with Feeling* (1988).

See also *Boro circles; Earth; Kakadu National Park; Oobarr; Warramurrungundji*.

Neil-loan See *Altair*.

Nerang See *Gold Coast*.

New moon Amongst the Wotjobaluk *Koori*, when children saw the new *moon*, they would form a circle, hold hands and call for it to grow. If it did not, they too would remain small.

See also *Death; Eclipse of the moon; First woman; Mityan the moon*.

Ngacu See *Bundjalung nation*.

Ngalyuka See *Eagle*.

Ngama Outcrop See *Yuendumu*.

Ngamba See *Bundjalung nation*.

Nganug See *Bralgu*.

Ngarang the swamp hawk See *Trickster character*.

Ngarinjin In 1956 the Ngarinjin people were collected, along with the Worora, at Mowanjum, a settlement just outside the town of Derby when their lands were flooded to create an artificial lake. Many ancestral tracks and *djang* sites were flooded by the waters.

Since then, they have been endeavouring to get some of their lands back. Their main ancestors are the *Wandjina*.

See also *Kimberley; Utemorrah, Daisy; Waterholes*.

Ngarluma and Jindjiparndi peoples The Ngarluma and Jindjiparndi peoples inhabit the mineral-rich area of the Pilbara, the central portion of Western Australia.

See also *Burrup Peninsula; Parraruru*.

Ngarugal the musk crow See *Trickster character*.

Ngawiya the sea turtle See *Great corroborees*.

Ngurunderi See *Island of the Dead; Sky world*.

Nimbin Nimbin is a small town in northern New South Wales important to the counter-culture and the practice of the healing arts. It is named after Nyimbunji, a strong and powerful *weeun*, or shaman, who had supernatural powers.

The place sacred to Nyimbunji is Nimbin Rocks and the area around it is still energized. Only initiated men and women wishing to become *shamans* or *weeun* would visit there. If they passed the tests they would attain shamanistic powers and could communicate with the spirit world on a high level. Stories connected with the rocks are very secret and are only to be told to those who have passed through all degrees of initiation.

See also *Dogs*.

Ninerung See *Dogs*.

Ningauis See *Kulama ceremonies*.

Nirunja See *Orion*.

Njimbun See *Jalgumbun*.

Noonkanbah Noonkanbah on the lower edge of the *Kimberley* region of Western Australia was—and remains—an important cultural and traditional centre for much of the area. It is surrounded by the tracks of the many *ancestral beings* of the *Dreamtime* or, in their language, the *Ngarranggani*. Around the central settlement are land features created by these ancestral beings and places where they emerged from or re-entered the ground. It is an area of many *djang* or, in their language, *malaji* sites.

In 1976, after years of struggle, the *Aboriginal* Yungngora and Kadjina communities regained the area from the previous white owners who had used it as a cattle station. They settled in happily and kept up the running of cattle on the property and enjoyed the freedom of their spiritual life. It was as if all the sacred sites had been returned to them. Yet this was only a mirage, for the Western Australian government, who had kept the mineral rights to the land, gave mining and drilling leases to international companies. During 1979 and 1980, the Noonkanbah *community*, with aid from all across Australia, fought to protect their sacred sites, but a convoy of police vehicles escorted a drilling rig onto the property and in August 1980 a test drilling was conducted near a sacred site called *Pea Hill*. No oil or minerals were found there, but the strength of the community was shattered. Aboriginal law had confronted white Australian law and white Australian law, backed up by force, had won. Because of the desecration of sacred ground, some of the *Aborigine* leaders, those who had been custodians of the site and had been active in the struggle, sickened and died. It is an example of what happens when material gain and indigenous spirituality clash.

Noonuccal people See *Oodgeroo*.

Nooralie See *All-Fathers*.

North-eastern Arnhem Land The people of north-eastern *Arnhem Land* have had contact with peoples outside Australia for many hundreds, if not thousands, of years, and these connections are recorded in long song circles. The Arnhem Landers, the Yolngu, divide all creation into two halves, or moieties, the *Duwa* and the *Yiritja*, a universal ordering which goes back to ancestral spirits from whom all the laws and customs governing the universe, animate and inanimate, come.

For the Duwa, among the great ancestors are the Djanggawul and the *Wawilak sisters*, for the Yiritja, *Barama and Laindjung*, but there are many other ancestral spirits who create the web of relationships which ordered life in the *Dreaming* as well as in the present. In Arnhem Land the trips they make are relatively short, as distinct from the long journeys of the desert ancestors, and the ancestors come from the sea to interact with the ancestral spirits already inhabiting the country. It is as if these myths contained in long elaborate song cycles detail the arrival of real people on the shores of Australia and their interactions with the locals.

See also *Bark paintings; Djanggawul mythology and ceremonies*.

No-yang the eel See *Frog*.

Numanirakala See *Mudungkala*.

Numuwuwari the giant crocodile ancestor was once a man who came from the country of stone. During a time of drought, he dived into a billabong and became a crocodile. *Crocodylus porosus*, the saltwater crocodile, reminds people of Numuwuwari, if he is their ancestor, when they see the reptile sunbaking on the mud flats or peering out of the water at them.

See also *Crocodiles*.

Nungar See *Nyungar*.

Nungeena See *Marmoo*.

Nyimbunji See *Bundjalung National Park; Dogs; Nimbin*.

Nyoongar See *Nyungar*.

Nyungar (or Nyoongar, Nunga) Nyungar is the collective name for the *Bibbulmum tribes* of south-western Australia.

See also *Bennell, Eddie; Community*.

Nyunggu See *Seagull and Torres Strait Pigeon*.

O

The origin of water

Olgas See *Katatjuta*.

Omens Omens, portents and warnings are conveyed to the *Aboriginal* people in a number of ways, through dreams, trances, unusual physical phenomena and strange behaviour in animals.
  See also *Shamans*.

Oobarr Oobarr in *Kakadu National Park* is a strong law place sacred to King Brown Snake or Irwardbad. *Bill Neidjie,* the custodian of the site, has said that it was King Brown Snake who made the *didjeridoo* and told everyone to use it in ceremonies. He represents the male principle and created Oobarr as a strong male centre. In the myth which Bill Neidjie relates, the rock python and her daughter die as a warning that women and uninitiated people are not allowed to go to Oobarr. There are equally strong female centres for Rock Python, who represents the female principle.

Oodgeroo (1920—93) was an elder of her people the Noonuccals and custodian of her country, the island of Minjerribah (Stradbroke Island) in the bay of Quandamooka (Moreton Bay). She lived at Moongalba (Old Woman's Place) and is well known for her teaching and spreading of *Aboriginal* culture. Unfortunately she died in 1993 while I was writing this book and about to go to see her, but I had already learnt much from her about the traditions of her land and enjoyed many a stay sitting at the campfire at Moongalba.

See also *Curlews; Dolphins; Rainbow snake; Southern Cross.*

Opals Opals, like other minerals, have a spiritual value in that they represent a part, such as an organ, a *Dreaming* ancestor left behind as a sign of his or her presence at a particular spot. Certain minerals and stones are imbued with the powerful energy of the ancestor.

The Adnyamathanha *elders* relate two stories about opals. The first is about a young boy who was chasing a kangaroo. He caught it at Minipa with his wooden club, then sat down to have a meal. While he ate, he stuck his club in the ground so that it stood up. The club turned into opal stone. This story refers to the vertical or oblique planes of rock in which opal is found, one end of which is on or near the surface.

The second story is about *Mambi the bronze-winged pigeon*, who threw a firestick high into the air. It landed near Cooper Pedy, an important opal mining area. When it came down and hit the ground sparks flew off in all directions. These became opals.

Origin of water See *Frog.*

Orion Orion is Nirunja, an important male figure in the *Pleiades* myth. He is engaged in an eternal chase after them and is still seen pursuing them in the sky.

The stars in his belt and scabbard are a group of young men, the Kulkunbulla, dancing a corroboree.

Otjout the cod fish See *Delphinus.*

Owl The owl is believed to be able to smell *death.* He is a watch bird for baneful spirits for, once aware of somone approaching death, he leads the baneful spirits there. Hence, his coming was a presage of death. This was the belief also for the mopoke.

Oyster and Shark The origin of the Oyster and Shark myth is related by an elder of the *Wik Munggan*. Once in the *Dreamtime* the Oyster brothers were sitting on the beach when they saw Shark cruising by after stingray. They called to him, but he did not reply. He returned eventually with a stingray and the brothers stole it from him. A fight ensured in which the shapes of oysters and sharks came about from the wounds inflicted on the combatants, for example the fin of the shark came from a *boomerang* lodged in his back. The oysters are flat because of being hit by the shark's spear thrower.

Oyster Cove Oyster Cove has become a sacred site for the Tasmanian *Kooris* as it is where many of their people died. In October 1847, 44 men, women and children, the remainder of the hundreds who had been exiled to Flinders Island in Bass Strait, were transferred to Oyster Cove and placed in an old penal settlement. At the end of 1854 only 3 men, 11 women and 2 boys remained. The people continued to decline and the last of the survivors, *Trugerninni*, died in 1876. A few other Tasmanian Aborigines who had managed to survive beyond the government protection became the ancestors of the present day Tasmanian Aborigines.

At Oyster Cove the Aborigines' presence can still be felt and it is an important place for the tribal revitalization occurring today among the Tasmanian Aborigines.

P

Pukamani funeral poles

Pakadringa See *Universe*.

Pakapaka See *Moiya and pakapaka*.

Palaneri See *Dreamtime*.

Palga Palga is a narrative *dance* style in the *Kimberley* region of Western Australia which has proved a source of continuing cultural vitality to the people of the region.

In 1974, Cyclone Tracy hit *Darwin*, smashing the city and leaving over 60 people dead or missing. It was interpreted by *Aboriginal* people as the anger of the *rainbow snake* who by this catastrophe warned them not to forsake their traditional law and ceremonies. Within a year, George Mangalamarra at Kalumburu had been given in dream the songs and dances of what came to be known as the 'Cyclone Tracy Palga'. This palga was performed regularly over the next two years throughout the Kimberley region.

Among the large painted headpieces or emblems held behind the heads of the performers were panels showing Unggud, the rainbow snake, and a long thread cross figure of the ancestral *Wandjina* as a serpent.

At the same time as this palga was being performed *Rover Thomas* of Warnum (Turkey Creek) was visited by the spirit of a woman who had died in a car accident. This *death* was seen to have been caused by another snake called Juntarkal. From this and similar visitations Rover Thomas created a palga called the 'Kuril Kuril'. The emblems of these dance sequences were eventually put on exhibition in Perth and caused an interest which led to Rover Thomas beginning to paint as an artist. His work is now much in demand.

Palkalina (*c.*1924) Palkalina was a shaman of the *Diyari people*. Although the making of a shaman in *Aboriginal* Australia is a secretive process about which not much is known, especially as to the ceremonies involved, Palkalina has left us a short account of the process:

He, the spirit, has many followers. During the daytime he is secretive, hiding in deep holes, creek beds, valleys, thickly-timbered country, deserted places. In the night-time he always walks, but does not do so during the day. When the weather is very hot, he goes into a *black* rain cloud. He is also secretly present in dust-storms, during thunder and is the mirage one often sees. He lives in hollow trees along with the bones of men. People are frightened of him when he walks about in the form of a bird. Only one person is safe from the spirit, the *kunki*, the shaman. And so I thought that I would get a kunki to show me his art. I could then be made one. Knowing that I am a powerful kunki, my people will esteem me.

Our kunki and I went to a place called Tipapilla. There we met a strange kunki who resembled the spirit. When I saw him, I shivered with great fear. Suddenly the spirit disappeared, but returned almost at once. I became very hungry. The first day of our seclusion in the bush, with the spirit, at Tipapilla, he gave me food that I had never had before. It was called *kujamara*, or 'spirit's food', which was native tobacco. He then read my thoughts, and saw that I desired to be made a kunki. He said that I should not think about other people, but only of the spirits. I then returned to my companion, the kunki. I spoke to him in a confused manner. He questioned me: 'What are you?' To which I replied, 'Many spirits.' He

then said, 'You are now a kunki. In time, I believe that you
will be a good one.'
  On the second day I went back into the bush and the spirit
came to me and performed certain rituals which I learned. I
then returned to my companion.

See also *Shamans*.

Papinjuwaris See *Cyclops*.

Papunya Papunya settlement was set up by the Australian
government in 1959 as a concentration settlement for the
Warlpiri, Luritja, Anmatyerre and Pinupi peoples, who were still
living their traditional life along the fringes of the *Western Desert*.
The people languished in the settlement under the *assimilation policy*, but in 1971, under the influence of a schoolteacher, Geoff
Bardon, the men began painting their traditional *Dreaming* stories
and this resulted in an explosion of what has come to be known as
the Papunya Tula style of *Aboriginal* art (see *Papunya Tula art*).
  With the demise of the assimilation policy and the struggle for
land rights which resulted in Land Rights legislation being passed
in the Northern Territory in 1976, the artificial settlement began
to wither away, with people going back to their traditional home-
lands. This has resulted in the spread of the Western Desert style
of acrylic art throughout the region.

Papunya Tula art Papunya Tula art is named after the settlement
of *Papunya* where this form of artwork began in the early 1970s
when men of the Walpiri began putting their *Dreaming* onto
boards and canvas using acrylic paint.
  The *Western Desert* has long been known for decorated boards
and stones known as *inma*, elaborate ceremonial decorations and
head-dresses and ground or sand paintings. Papunya Tula art
makes use of many symbols and designs, which change their
meanings according to the context in which they are used. The
most common symbols are the circle—which can mean a waterhole or campsite among other things—and the sinuous line or
lines representing a path, track or stream. The symbols are used to
tell stories of the *Dreamtime* and the ancestors. They are also
stylized maps of certain parts of the country belonging to the
artist.
  The pictorial style is distinguished by the use of dots to create
surface patterns and visual texture. This is a direct extension of

sand painting, in which small particles of matter such as coloured down, pulped seeds or plants, as well as ochres and other material, are used to form an elaborate pattern on the ground similar to an 'installation' (see *Ground paintings*). I remember in 1988 seeing in Western Australia an installation formed from such material by a desert artist, a Wonghi.

The Papunya movement has produced a number of famous artists, such as Clifford Possum Tjapaltjarri, and has spread through much of the Western Desert, with different styles being produced though using the same dot techniques.

Parachilna Parachilna is an important *red ochre* deposit in South Australia. According to myth, it is where the dog and gecko fought, and the blood of the dying dog turned into an ochre deposit.

The Adnyamathanha *elders* narrate how in the *Flinders Range* in South Australia there lived a gecko lizard named Adno-artina. Every day he would climb a high peak and challenge everyone to do battle. Marindi the giant dog heard his challenge. He bounded up the valley towards the gecko, barking his answer. Adno-artina looked at the giant dog, at his huge jaws and pointed teeth, and decided to play the trickster.

'I'll fight you later,' he said.

Marindi growled, 'Yes, you'll make a meal for my puppies.' He curled up at the base of the hill and went to sleep.

Adno-artina waited until dark, then he issued his challenge again and, just to make sure that he would not lose his courage, he tied a magic string about his tail. Marindi leapt up and tried to seize Gecko by the back of his neck to shake the life from him, but Gecko was too quick. He ran in beneath the dog's slavering jaws, seized the dog by the throat and hung on. Marindi tried to shake the lizard off, but could not. The sharp teeth ripped into his throat, red blood spouted out and formed the red ochre deposit found at Parachilna today.

Marindi, the dog of this myth, appears to be one of the Melatji Law Dogs whose *Dreaming tracks* start and stop over much of Australia.

See also *Dogs; Giant dogs*.

Parraruru (Robert Churnside; ?–1970s) Parraruru was an elder of the *Ngarluma people* and a great story-teller and singer of traditional songs in the form called *djabi*. He was a fountain of tribal knowledge, some of which has been preserved in the Institute of *Aboriginal* and Islander Studies in Canberra, the capital of

Australia.
   See also *Burrup Peninsula*.

Pea Hill (Umpampurru) is an important sacred site to the
Aboriginal community of *Noonkanbah*. It was here that the creative
hero Unyupu and the two snakes he fought went to *earth*. In their
fight they had carved out the Fitzroy river. The battlefield was
crossed by the track of Nangala, the pregnant wife of the giant
Jangalajarra snake, in her travels north to her final resting-place.
Then Looma the blue tongue lizard woman stopped here on her
journey in a north-westerly direction to her final resting-place on
a small hill overlooking the Looma Aboriginal community.
Through these associations Pea Hill became a powerful *djang* or
malaji site and is the *djang* place of a powerful female spirit.
   Pea Hill is also the *djang* place for snakes, *frogs* and goannas.
The ritual expert responsible for the site can open the hill and
enter it, providing the female spirit custodian there permits it.
Inside, he approaches her and urges her to see to the propagation
of snakes, frogs and goannas. At one place on the hill goannas are
summoned from the surrounding area and placed within the hill.
At certain times these goannas are released from the hill to keep
up the species and provide a food source.
   Pea Hill was also the keeping-place for a number of sacred
objects (including *inma* boards) and thus it was important for a
number of reasons. There was much consternation in the community when in 1980 an area nearby was drilled in the search for
minerals and oil. In spite of a nationwide protest the drilling was
allowed, with a resulting loss of confidence in Aboriginal customs,
laws and spirituality (see *Noonkanbah*).

Pearl shell ornaments Pearl shell ornaments were used in north-
western Australia as a pubic covering or decoration by youths
undergoing initiation. At the conclusion of the ceremonies, they
were traded over the western half of the continent south to the
coasts of the Great Australian Bight. Many of these shell ornaments were decorated with an interlocking key pattern.
   See also *Initiation process; Trade*.

Peewit In *Cape York peninsula* a myth is related about two birds,
Peewit and *Willy Wagtail*, who quarrelled because Peewit's wife,
the waterlily woman, was having an affair with the willy wagtail.
They came to blows and fought with burning ashes. Peewit was
badly burnt in the fight. At last they stopped and talked things
over and decided to go to their respective *djang* places. Now the

peewit and willy wagtail have *black* feathers from the fight and the peewit sits aloft in a tree where he can see all around and call out a warning when he sees wives who are being unfaithful to their husbands.

Pemulwuy (1760?–1802) Pemulwuy was a leader of the *Eora tribe* who fought against the British invasion at Sydney. He was murdered and his head cut off. It was pickled in a barrel and sent to England as a sign that the Eora nation had been conquered.

Perth See *Bennell, Eddie; Bennett's Brook; Bropho, Robert; Crow; Dreaming tracks; Palga; Shamans; Trade; Wagyal; Yagan.*

Pigeon See *Jandamara.*

Pike, Jimmy Jimmy Pike, a well known *Aboriginal* artist, was born in the Great Sandy Desert during the Second World War. He was one of the last *Walmatjarri people* to leave the desert in the 1950s.

Pikuwa See *Crocodiles.*

Pilbara region See *Aboriginal and Aborigine; Burrup peninsula; Millstream pools; Ngarluma and Jindjiparndi peoples; Warmalana.*

Pinjarra See *Yagan.*

Pintoma See *Kulama ceremonies.*

Pipeclay See *White ochre.*

Pitchuri See *Pituri.*

Pitipituis See *Mudungkala.*

Pituri (or Pitchuri) (*Duboisia hopwoodii*), also called 'native tobacco', was an important drug. It was used as a stimulant and intoxicant by older *Aboriginal* men, especially during long ceremonies. In some areas it was used in initiation ceremonies in the making of *shamans*, where it was used to make the initiate sensitive to the presence of spirits. It was traded over a large area of Australia.

Platypus Amongst the Kabi Kabi people of Queensland there is the myth that once Platypus were *dinderi* (little men) who travelled along the Brisbane river catching and eating water snake. They travelled from place to place and lagoon to lagoon until they reached Mairwan Lagoon, where the water snakes managed to overpower them and turn them into the first platypus.

Pleiades (*Kungkarangkalpa*) The Pleiades are an important group of stars which form the basis of a similar myth all across Australia. They represent a group of young women, seven sisters, who are pursued by *Orion*. In the desert communities, this is considered a woman's myth, though the group of women have connections with many of the other *ancestral beings* belonging to men's business.

In the desert area around Kalgoorlie, it is related that once the seven sisters decided to visit the *Earth* and flew down. They looked for their favourite plateau to land on; but found their landing-place covered with little men called Yayarr. They called to them to get out of the way, but they refused. The sisters finally landed upon another hill. The Yayarr men saw where they landed and decided to capture them. The sisters ran off and eventually the men grew tired of the pursuit, except for one. He kept on following them and following them. At last one of the sisters left the group to find water. The man followed her. She found water and was drinking it when she heard the faint sound of a foot being placed carefully on the ground. She looked up, saw the Yayarr man and raced off. He charged after her and finally caught her. She yelled and screamed. He picked up a stick to quieten her and swung it. The woman jumped out of the way. He swung the stick again and again and missed and missed. The marks of his stick can still be seen on the side of a hill in that country. Finally, the woman escaped back to the hill where she and her sisters had landed. They had gone. She looked up into the sky, saw her six sisters there and rose to join them. The Yayarr man followed after and became Orion.

When the Pleiades are seen at dawn, it is said that this is a sign that the cold season is coming.

See also *Aldebaran; Crow; Emu; Sirius; Two Men myth; Western Desert*.

Pompey See *Jinabuthina*.

Pukamani burial poles A unique feature of the *Tiwi people's Pukamani funeral ceremonies* is the planting of a number of decorated and carved poles in the ground which after the service are left to decay. A wide variety of designs are used and the shapes of the poles are said to be stylized sculptures of forks or limbs of trees, breasts of women, rocks on the sea-coast and windows and doors (the pieces cut out from the poles). The symbols painted on the poles refer to the landscape of the island and many other things such as certain species of fauna and flora.

Sometimes one of the burial poles is in the shape of a human being and this is placed at the head of the grave. This is because when the soul leaves the grave he will see the sculpture and, thinking it a living being, will stop to talk to it, saying farewell before he goes on his way.

See also *Bark paintings; Tree between Heaven and Earth.*

Pukamani funeral ceremonies The Pukamani funeral service is an elaborate series of ceremonies which were first performed in the *Dreamtime* for the ancestral hero Purukupali, the man who brought *death* into the world when his son Djinini died. When a relative, Tukimbini, heard of this, he sent a message stick to Talinini of the *honey* people of Bathurst Island, appointing him the ceremonial leader of the burial rituals. Those who lived nearby he made workers. It was their duty to cut the burial poles which are a feature of this ceremony (see *Pukamani burial poles*), make and paint the large ceremonial baskets and the elaborate pukamani *spears* as well as to clear the burial ground near where Purukupali had entered the sea and drowned (there was therefore no grave to keep clean as is the case when there is a body).

The party who cut the poles consisted of fresh water, *fire*, honey-eater, saw-fish, mosquito, shark and mullet men. Two turtle women made the large baskets and a honey woman made another basket which was decorated by two honey men. With the working party engaged in their tasks, Talinini sent specially carved message sticks to the various groups of people on *Melville Island* and Bathurst Island. They were to assemble at certain places, then move to Tapararimi where the funeral service was to take place. Along the way they were to perform the preliminary *ilania* ceremonies—ceremonies dealing with the ancestors which led up to the final funeral ceremonies.

The groups of people came together at Rulijunga, where they performed another *ilania* before going to the final place. After a ceremonial fight between the visitors and the workers, who were seen as *mopaditis*, spirits of the dead, the final ceremonies were performed at the burial ground where five pukamani poles had been erected. Everyone decorated themselves and both men and women moved to the grave.

The end of this first funeral service also marked the end of the Dreamtime. The mythical or Dreamtime ancestors returned to their camps and transformed themselves into the various birds, fish, reptiles, heavenly bodies and inanimate objects of the present. The first Pukamani funeral service was thus more than a service for Purukupali. It was also a service for the ending the Dreamtime period and the advent of a new age. It is this aspect which is still remembered in the elaborate rituals which accompany the sending off of the deceased.

See also *Curlews; Dhambidj song series of Arnhem Land*.

Pulpul See *Burrup Peninsula*.

Pungalunga men The Pungalunga men were cannibal giants who lived in the *Dreamtime*. They hunted human beings for food and returned to their camp with the bodies tucked in their *hair string* belts. They were destroyed after the great battle at *Uluru* when they allied themselves with the vanquished in a bid for revenge. Only one giant was left and some accounts say the shape of *Katatjuta* is that of the heads of the animals and humans he killed.

One day the remaining giant Pungalunga came across the camp of mice women who had never seen a man before. Pungalunga asked them why there were no men about and the leader of the mice women, who was taller and larger than the others, replied that she hadn't known that men existed until he came along. 'What are men for?' she innocently asked. 'I'll show you,' he replied and grabbed and raped her. The mice woman screamed and bit him on the lip. All the other mice women started shouting and, as they continued, turned into *dogs*, or dingoes, and attacked him. He struggled to fight them off, for although he had killed many animals before—emus, kangaroos and wallabies—he had never been attacked by dogs. Finally he turned and ran off in a panic. The dogs followed, snapping at his heels. Pungalunga calmed down as he ran and saw a tree in front of him. He pulled it from the ground, rubbed off the branches and bent it into the shape of a *boomerang*. He turned, confronted the pack, smashed the boomerang into their faces and, one by one, knocked out their teeth. At long last the toothless dogs turned and ran off. Pungalunga's battle with the mice women took place at Katatjuta and there they may be seen in the features of the rock formations. At the bottom of a cliff are huge boulders which are said to be Pungalunga's bones.

Purra the kangaroo See *Beehive; Two Brothers*.

Purukupali See *Curlew; Mundungkala; Pukamani funeral ceremonies*.

Purutjikini See *Kulama ceremonies*.

Q

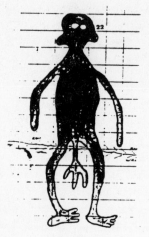

Quinkin spirit

Quartz crystal Quartz crystal is said to be possessed of magic properties and when a shaman is made he receives an empowered piece of crystal which he keeps hidden and away from the eyes of the uninitiated. Not only is it used in harmful processes such as *bone pointing*, but also in effecting cures. The shaman rubs or presses the crystal over the affected part, while chanting a spell. He then sucks the part and extracts a foreign body which is the cause of the trouble. This may be a slither of bone, stone or wood.

See also *Marnbi the bronze-winged pigeon; Shamans*.

Quinkin (or Quinkan; Kwinkin; Kwinkan) are spiritual embodiments of lust, symbolized by the male sexual organ. They are depicted in the rock galleries at *Laura, Cape York peninsula*, northern Queensland, with very large and often misshapen penises.

Once in the *Dreamtime*, Tul-Tul the plover went hunting, leaving his wife and son in camp. Ungarr, one of the Quinkin, watched the camp and became aroused when he saw the woman pounding pandanus nuts with her legs apart. He crept up, pushed her over and pushed his long penis into her. It was so long that it went right through and out of her mouth. She died and Ungarr in dismay went to hide in his home, a tall, hollow, dead tree.

Tul-Tul was very upset when he found his wife dead, but he brought her back to life and healed her. To exact vengeance on the Quinkin, he went to the hollow tree, cut a hole in the bottom and filled it with grass and sticks. Ungarr heard him and asked what he was doing, but Tul-Tul said that he was only making the hollow tree proof against the elements. He blocked all the other holes in the tree with pieces of bark, then lit the grass and sticks at the bottom of the trunk. Ungarr was burnt to ashes, except for his very long penis, which was too hard to burn. Tul-Tul chopped it up into little pieces, then threw them all around the country so that each man and woman received a piece. This is how men and women first received their penises and clitorises.

See also *Mimi spirits*.

R

Rainbow snake

Rain-making According to Aboriginal myth, clouds are inhabited by spirits or a spirit which controls not only the rain, but wind, thunder and *lightning*. In asking for rain the shaman directly invokes the aid of this spirit by the performance of a rain-making ritual. He calls on the spirit to give him power to make the rain fall, while whirring a *bull-roarer*. Goanna fat is rubbed on a youth's body and causes steam to rise, which is said to rise to make rain clouds. The ceremony takes place in a hut in which the *elders* and the shaman sit. The shaman cuts his arms and soaks up the blood with down, which is then thrown into the air. There are large stones in the hut which represent clouds. After the ceremony is over, these stones are placed in a tree and powdered gypsum is thrown into a waterhole. When these ritual actions are completed, clouds gather in the sky. The ceremony concludes with the pulling down of the hut.

See also *Akurra serpent; Bundjalung National Park; Floods; Great flood; Monsoon; Taipan; Thalu places.*

Rainbow snake The rainbow snake is perhaps the most important deity in *Aboriginal* Australia, being connected with not only all snake ancestors, but also such important All-Father deities as *Biame* and the *Wandjina* ancestors of the *tribes* of the *Kimberley* region of Western Australia. The rainbow serpent is also the giver as well as the guardian of the mystic healing rites of the *shamans*. *Oodgeroo*, an elder of the Noonuccal *community*, whose ancestral land is the island of Minjerribah in Moreton Bay close to Brisbane, Queensland, makes her the primordial deity of all life, an All-Mother.

See also *Akurra serpent; All-Fathers; All-Mothers; Bennett's Brook; Bolung; Boomerang; Bunyip; Jarapiri; Katatjuta; Kulunbar; Menstrual blood; Monsoon; Palga; Wagyal; Warramurrungundji*.

Rangga *Rangga* are the sacred objects of the Yolngu people of *Arnhem Land*. They are highly decorated poles which were given to the various clans in the *Dreamtime* by ancestral and cultural beings. They are similar to *inma* and *tjuringa* sacred objects and have the same or similar powers.

See also *Barama and Laindjung myths; Djanggawul mythology and ceremonies; Duwa moiety; Rom ceremony of Arnhem Land*.

Red, black, yellow and white are the sacred colours which were given to the *Aborigines* during the *Dreamtime* and, among many other things, represent the four elements. *Black* is the *earth*, but, more, it is the marks of the campfires where the ancestors camped on the earth during the Dreamtime; red is blood, energy and *fire*, and represents the *djang*, the power found in the strong places of the earth; yellow represents liquid, water and the marks on the back of the great snake ancestor; white represents the sky, the air and the stars, and symbolizes those ancestors who after their work was done ascended into the sky, where they wink down at the Earth as stars (see *Stars and constellations*).

See also *Earth, water, fire and air; Red ochre; White ochre; Yellow ochre*.

Red flying foxes See *Flying foxes*.

Red ochre (*Wiltja*) is the most sacred of colours. In central Australia it is said to be the blood shed by Marindi the dog who died when he fought Adno-artina the gecko lizard at *Parachilna* in South Australia. The red ochre was considered so powerful here that it was traded far and wide.

Red ochre is often reserved for sacred ceremonies, whereas the *white ochre*, or pipeclay, may be used for what are called open ceremonies.

Red is a sacred colour of the *Duwa moiety* of *Arnhem Land*.

See also *Bark paintings; Great battles; Gunabibi ceremonies; Ingelaladd; Initiation process; Mimi spirits; Morning Star; Red, black, yellow and white; Sun; Taboo countries; Yellow ochre.*

Red waratah The red waratah tree is the official emblem of the state of New South Wales and there is a legend of the *Eora tribe* to explain how it turned from white to red.

In the *Dreamtime* the Wonga Pigeon ancestor camped with her mate. One day, he went hunting and failed to return. She could not find him and was attacked by a hawk. She was wounded, but escaped and hid among the branches of a waratah. She heard her mate calling and tried to fly to him. Weak from loss of blood, she fluttered through the waratah and her blood stained the blossoms, turning them red.

Relics of the dead Relics of a dead person were highly venerated by a number of *Aboriginal* groups, including those of *Tasmania*. There a skull or bone of a venerated elder was carried and communicated with when problems arose.

Bone relics of *shamans* were especially held in great esteem by other shamans, who might use them in healing and harming rituals.

See also *Death*.

Rigel To the Wotjobaluk *Kooris* the star Rigel was Yerrerdet-kurrk, the mother of Totyerguil (*Altair*)'s two wives. She never allowed her son-in-law to see her and thus was a visible symbol of the *mother-in-law avoidance* taboo.

See also *Murray river*.

Rober Carol The star Rober Carol was considered to be the wife of Waa (*Crow*) who became the star *Canopus*. The smaller stars around her were their children.

Roberts, Tulo See *Great corroborees*.

Rock engravings Rock engravings are by far the most ancient works of *Aboriginal* artists. These extend all over the continent, ranging from isolated carvings to huge galleries on expanses of flat rock.

In the Hawkesbury river area of New South Wales, large carved figures of male ancestors are said to be those of *Biame*, the All-Father deity of that area.

See also *Ground carvings and sculptures; Rock paintings*.

Rock paintings Rock paintings are found in many places in Australia. Many of them are thousands of years old and from them we may see how our ancestors lived. They are, however, still being painted today. *Laura* (the famous Quinkan country) in northern Queensland and *Kakadu National Park* are places where fine examples of rock art may be seen.

See also *Bark paintings; Kuringgai Chase National Park; Marwai the master painter; Mimi spirits; Rock engravings; Yuendumu*.

Roe, Paddy Paddy Roe is a Nyigina man who lives in Broome, Western Australia. He is an elder and ceremonial leader and some of his stories have been published in *Gularabulu*, edited by Stephen Muecke.

See also *Animal behaviour; Trickster character*.

Rom ceremony of Arnhem Land The Rom ceremony is a diplomatic ceremony which was performed in *Arnhem Land* to establish or reaffirm friendly relations between people of different communities and often of different *languages* and cultures. At the core of the ceremony is the presentation of a bound and decorated pole by a visiting group of singers and dancers in response to an invitation from a prominent member of the host *community*.

Like the funeral services, the Rom ceremonies are based on *manikay* or a song series. Requests for Rom ceremonies are often sent to renowned singers and may be accompanied by a token of sincerity, such as the umblicus of the sponsor's child, or the sponsor may send skeins of banyan string to bind the pole.

The *rangga*, the Rom pole, has a special association with one of the *wangarr*, spirit beings or ancestors, such as Wild Honey in Djambidji or *Morning Star* in Goyulan. The preparation of the pole takes place in a bough shade, an open framework which is roofed by leafy boughs to keep the sun off while the pole is being decorated, and is accompanied by the singing of many sacred songs. After arriving at the community of the hosts, the visitors construct the bough shade on the outskirts of the community, where the pole is hidden from view, and each evening they perform *dances* selected from the manikay repertoire such as 'White Cockatoo', 'King

Brown Snake' and so on.

On the penultimate day, the performers bring out the Rom pole and carry it through the hosts' camp, pausing at various points to dance. The performances continue in a central place until late at night.

The following morning the visitors carry the Rom pole to the camp of the sponsor and in a grand performance formally present it to him in the presence of the combined crowd of hosts and visitors.

A Rom ceremony was held in Canberra, the capital of Australia, in November 1982.

Roughsey, Dick (?–1985) Goolbalathaldin, or Dick Roughsey, as he was more commonly known, was a Lardil man from *Mornington Island* off *Cape York peninsula* in the far north of Australia. He was well known as a story-teller and artist and published a number of *Aboriginal* myths rewritten as children's stories.

See also *Giant dogs*.

Roughsey, Elsie See *Labumore*.

S

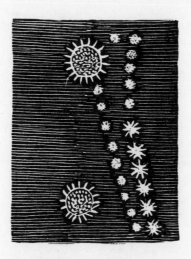

Stars and constellations

Sacred places These are strong (*djang*) *earth* places which have been sanctified and energized by the ancestors in the *Dreamtime*. They are connected by the *Dreaming tracks* or *song lines* and are like beads scattered along a thread. They have been described as giant batteries which are constantly giving out energy to keep all species strong and on-going. To destroy them is to destroy some of the earth energy, and thus weaken all that live and breathe. They also have been seen as nodes of energy along the telluric power lines that crisscross the earth.

See also *Auwa; Djang; Secret/sacred information; Thalu places; Walkabout*.

Sagittarius Two stars in Sagittarius were two of the *moeity ancestor Bunjil's* young men, Tadjeri the brush-tailed possum and Tarnung the gliding phalanger. They represented moeity sections, or clans.

Scorpio The constellation of Scorpio recounts in the sky the penalty for the breaking of the law which forbade a newly initiated man from having sexual relations with women until after he was purified.

A young initiate was seduced by a girl and when they were discovered they escaped into the sky. The young man's two teachers followed closely. They flung *boomerangs* and clubs at the couple, but missed. All of them then became stars. One teacher is the second magnitude star Shauld in the tail of Scorpio and the other teacher is the star close by. The young man and woman are the two small paired stars to the right. The headband of the youth, which he lost in his flight and which symbolizes his failure to complete the initiation ceremonies, is the star cluster just below the constellation. It is said that he is vainly trying to regain his headband, but is held back by his lover.

See also *Initiation process*.

Seagull and Torres Strait Pigeon Seagull (Sivri) and Torres Strait Pigeon (Nyunggu) are cultural heroes of the Tyongandyi clan of the *Wik Munggan* people.

It is told that Sivri and Nyunggu once lived on opposite sides of the river Langanama. To Sivri's clan belonged all the seagulls, the cockatoos, the crocodile, the crabs and different fishes. To Nyunggu's clan belonged the white pigeon, the native companion, the *black* duck the crane and other birds. His daughters are said to be the small mussell shell, the bailer shell, pearl shell and conch shell.

Sivri was always dancing. In fact, he did nothing but *dance*. He created the drum for his dances and made many songs. He made the first bow and arrow; he made the first *canoes*.

Nyunggu used to send his daughters to get water from the river and they saw Sivri and wanted him. They made signs for him to come to their side of the river. One day he got into his canoe and paddled to Nyunggu's side of the river and climbed a big tea-tree. The women found him there. He put them into his canoe and pushed off onto the river. He went downstream and left one woman who had a sore breast on an island and another on another island where his canoe ran aground. He continued on his journey, walking on the sea. Where he placed his feet islands and sandbanks came up. He made all the islands of the Torres Strait.

Nyunggu followed in pursuit of Sivri to get his daughters back, but he missed him and continued on into Papua New Guinea where he is to this day. There he taught the people his songs and dances. Sivri himself ended up on Maubiyag Island where he taught the people there his songs and dances. He remains there to this day.

Seasons The *Bibbulmum* people divided the year into six seasons. Summer was *birok*; early and late autumn were *burnoru* and *geran*; winter was *maggoro*; and early and late spring were *kambarang* and *jilba*.

In the far North, the Bunitj people also divided their year into six seasons based on the seasonal changes. These were: *Gunumeleng* (October–December), the pre-monsoonal season; *Gudjewg* (January–March), the monsoonal season with its heavy rain; *Bang-Gereng* (April), the end of the rains; *Yegge* (May–June), the drying-out season; *Wurrgeng* (June–July), the cool season; *Gurrung* (August–September), the hot, dry season.

See also *Monsoon*.

Secret/sacred information Many of the ceremonies and songs of *Aboriginal* Australia are owned by those initiated into the particular cults built around ancestral figures. With age, a person gains more and more information about the ancestors from the *elders*.

Because of certain land rights laws under which Aboriginal people must prove their ownership of their own land, often they are forced, to their distress, to reveal secret or sacred information to uninitiated people. This happens also in regard to *sacred places*, many of which should remain secret, not only to protect them, but also to protect persons from the energy stored there.

Shamans (*bulyaguttuk; maban; mekigar; urngi; weeun; wirnum* and other names, depending on the language of the particular group)

A shaman is a man or woman who has received the shamanic calling, usually in a dream. His duties are: mediating in quarrels; offering advice; foretelling coming events; healing; counteracting negative forces, including inimical magic; and also practising what may be termed 'black magic', including *bone pointing*.

Entering a trance state is an ability which many, if not all, *Aboriginal* shamans have. During these trances shamans meet spirits, cure patients and fly to the *sky world*. They also receive (dream) new songs and ceremonies.

Balbuk, a *yorga binderr* or strong woman, was a shaman of the Nyungar of Perth at the end of the nineteenth century. Her duties consisted of settling quarrels and stopping feuds between families, foretelling the success of the hunt and smoking magic into a spear or dog to ensure good hunting. She prophesized from signs such as the falling of a leaf, the snapping of a twig, a bird's cry or the motions of a whirlwind, or Willy Willy.

The Kurnai *Koori* people of Victoria had two kinds of shaman: Birraarks and Mullamulluns. Birraarks were the magicians who practised magic and made shamanistic journeys to the sky world, bringing back ceremonies. One of these Birraarks, Bunjil Narran (Master Moon), whilst flying across Lake Wellington, is supposed to have released his grip on the magic cord which shamans used in flying and other feats. He was saved by the spirits accompanying him on his flight.

Mullamulluns were closer to doctors—they knew the properties of herbs and practised the healing arts such as *smoking*, massaging and removing small objects such as quartz splinters from the body of a sick person.

Whilst in the sky world shamans were not supposed to laugh and had to remain serious. To maintain their powers on *Earth*, they did not eat any part of a kangaroo with blood on it and they could not kill human beings.

See also *Akurra serpent; Animal behaviour; Australites; Bunjil; Dorubauk; Dreaming; Dreaming tree of life; Extinct giant marsupials; Fire; Jalgumbun; Jandamara; Kutji spirits; Mundjauin; Nyimbunji; Omens; Palkalina; Pituri; Quartz crystal; Rain-making; Rainbow serpent; Relics of the dead; Spirit snake; Taipan; Tree between Heaven and Earth; Tuurap Warneen; Two Brothers; White Lady; Wirnum.*

Shields Wooden shields were part of the equipment of most male *Aborigines*. They were usually made from hardwood and were quite narrow, being used to batter aside *spears* rather than letting them strike full on. Some of these shields were engraved with abstract designs.

In Queensland, the shields were larger and made from a light soft wood. Often they were over a metre in length and painted with clan designs in red, yellow and white.

Sickness country See *Taboo countries*.

Sirius For the *Koori* Mara people the star Sirius was the female wedge-tail eagle, Gneeanggar, who was carried off by Waa the *crow* (*Canopus*). This myth also involves the *Pleiades* who are seen by the Mara as seven young women. They lived together and did not want to be separated. Gneeanggar was one of them. Crow saw her, fell in love with her and decided to kidnap her. Once the seven sisters were out looking for witchetty grubs. They were very fond of the white flesh of this succulent grub. Waa saw them and immediately transformed himself into a grub and bored into a tree. The sisters found his hole and each in turn tried to hook him out with the small hooked stick which is used for this purpose. As each woman pushed her hook down, he broke it off. However, when Gneeanggar pushed her hook down the hole, he allowed himself to be hooked and drawn out. As she was raising him to her mouth, he turned back to a crow and carried her off to the sky where she became Sirius. He became the star Canopus. The six remaining sisters went into the sky as the Pleiades and are still looking for their sister.

See also *Taboo countries*.

Sivri See *Seagull and Torres Strait Pigeon*.

Skin groups See *Kin groups*.

Skipper, Peter (born *c.*1929) Peter Skipper is an artist and story-teller of the *Walmatjarri people* who now live at Fitzroy Crossing. His totem or *Dreaming* is the barn *owl*. He has had a number of major exhibitions of his work.

Sky world The sky world is a world above the *Earth*.

Among the Lower *Murray river* people, the *elders* tell how the ancestral hero Ngurunderi began his long trek to the sky world of the dead, going towards the setting *sun*. He took his sons with him. On the way, one of his sons became lost, leaving one of his *spears* behind him. Ngurunderi tied a cord to the butt of the spear and threw it into the air. It homed in on the missing boy, who was drawn back to his father. This *Dreaming* story explains what hap-pened to the soul after a person had died: it was drawn to its final home in the sky where it was received with great rejoicing and lived on happily ever after.

See also *Australites; Biame; Bunjil; Cosmography; Curlews; Death; Dreaming tree of life; Emu; Extinct giant marsupials; Galaxy; Island of the dead; Matchwood tree; Mundjauin; Narroondarie; Shamans; Spirit snake; Tree between Heaven and Earth; Two Brothers; Underworld; Universe*.

Sleeping giant There is a myth of a sleeping giant among the Yuggera people of Queensland whose country is near the town of Ipswich. The giant is identified with Mount Castle. He is an All-Father figure which has been identified with *Biame*. He is described as an old man who has been lying asleep with his head resting on the palm of one hand with the elbow buried deep within the ground. In the *Dreamtime*, the giant awoke and flooded the whole country, but now he is sleeping again until the time comes to awaken and go to the aid of his people.

See also *All-Fathers; Luma Luma the giant*.

Smoking Smoking is an important purifying ritual for birth, sickness and to purify houses in which a *death* has occurred. It forms part and the conclusion of many important ceremonies.

See also *Eaglehawk and crow; Herbal medicines; Initiation process; Shamans*.

Solomon, James See *Bindirri, Yirri*.

Solomon, Roger See *Bindirri, Yirri*.

Song lines Song lines are the sound equivalents of the spacial journeys of the ancestors, the lines of which are found also inscribed in *Aboriginal* paintings and carvings. They detail the travels of the ancestors and each verse may be read in terms of the geographical features of the landscape. Encoded within them are the great ceremonies which reactivate the *Dreamtime* in the present.

See also *Australian indigenous mythology; Kulunbar; Sacred places; Wagyal; Walkabout*.

Southern Cross The Southern Cross constellation has many myths attached to it. Among the *Koori* people of Victoria the star at the head of the Cross was Bunya. He was pursued by Tjingal the *emu* and in panic threw his *spears* down at the foot of a tree and ran up it for safety. He became a possum. The eastern stars in the Cross were two spears thrown by the Bram-Bram-Bult brothers, who were two stars in the forelegs of *Centaurus*. The larger star of the Cross was the spear which struck Tjingal on the chest, and the smaller star was the spear which passed through his neck. The star at the bottom of the Cross was the spear which hit him in the haunches. The west star of the Cross was Druk the *frog*, the mother of the Bram-Bram-Bult.

Another myth was narrated by *Oodgeroo* of the Noonuccal people of Minjerribah (Stradbroke Island). According to this myth, the Southern Cross was a special creation of the All-Father *Biame*. It is the gum-tree named Yaraando, the *Dreaming tree of life* and *death*. The stars of the Cross are the eyes of a man imprisoned in the tree, blazing in the darkness. The stars called the 'pointers' are two white cockatoos that flew after the tree when it was lifted into the sky. It is a visible symbol of the hereafter and of the All-Father Biame.

For many *Aboriginal* communities along the eastern coast the Southern Cross is a protector spirit, Mirrabooka. He was placed in the sky by the All-Father *Biame*, who gave him lights for his hands and feet and stretched him across the sky so that he might forever watch over his people. The pointers are his eyes.

See also *Djamar; Galaxy*.

Southern Lights See *Aurora Australis*.

Spear throwers See *Flying foxes*.

Spears Spears, the chief weapons of the *Aboriginal* people of Australia, were given to men in the *Dreamtime*.

The *Wik Munggan elders* narrate how some of the first spears came from Kongkong the fishhawk. This myth is well worth relating in detail, as it contains not only the first making of the spear but also other motifs which are found in myths world-wide. It also contains aspects of Wik Munggan culture which have since died out or been heavily modified under the influence of Christianity.

Kongkong (Fishhawk) and his son went to make spears. They made all kinds of spears: *wolka*, a stingray-barbed spear; *kaiya*, with a cluster of stingray barbs; *antyan*, a spear with four prongs; *yandala*, with one long point; *tu'u* and *wantyandyindan*, with three prongs for spearing bony bream fish; *pinta*, a bamboo spear with one point; and *pita*, a spear with four points. They also made spear throwers and fighting clubs. They tied the spears up in a bundle and put them in the branch of a tree and they did the same with their spear throwers and clubs.

It was then that Rock Python asked his son to go and visit Fishhawk. He went and along the way met his two sisters. Leaving them, he continued on his way and reached the camp of Fishhawk, but it was deserted. He found the weapons and took them back to the camp of his two sisters, giving them to the women to look after.

Meanwhile Kongkong and his son returned to find the weapons gone. Kongkong saw tracks and identified them as belonging to the son of Rock Python. He told his son to follow the tracks. He did so and entered the camp of the two women. They gave him food and firewood and he camped there. Next morning, he woke up and saw the women still asleep. He called to them, but they didn't move. He came closer and had intercourse with the elder while she slept. When they woke up, the younger sister saw the marks of the rape on her elder sister's body. They decided to avenge the outrage. Taking up the spears and spear throwers, they rushed after Kongkong's son. They began throwing spears but he kept striking them aside. Then the younger sister threw a spear. It pierced him in the thigh. She speared him in the breast with a four-pronged spear. He fell. The sisters speared him dead, cut off both legs and arms, then cut his throat. They carried him back to their camp.

Young Sister said, 'Older sister, bring me an ant-bed.'

Elder Sister replied, 'Younger sister, aren't you glad to do the cooking? There'll be so much meat.'

They cooked the meat (as birds are cooked) in ant-bed, then erected a platform on forked sticks on which to place the meat. After this, they sat down and put on mourning ashes for the 'brother' who had been slain.

Meanwhile Kongkong the father had vomited and felt that it was a sign that something had happened to his son. He followed the tracks calling for his son, 'Kong, kong, kong.' At last he reached the two sisters' camp and saw the platform and beneath it the sisters covered in mourning ashes.

'You have killed my son,' he said, adding that he would not retaliate. However, he set up camp beside them, waited until they were off guard and speared them both.

After he had killed them, he cut their bodies into two pieces and then, taking his spears, went off to his old father and mother. He got into a canoe with his father and mother and they paddled off. In the middle of the stream, the canoe swirled around and Kongkong said, 'Mother, father, let us descend into our sacred place.'

The canoe capsized and they all sank, except for Kongkong who flapped his wings and flew off as a bird. He flew back to the platform where the meat of his son had been placed and built his nest there. From there he called, 'Mother, father, stay below. I'll stay up here.'

His father and mother now remain in the water as catfish and one can see the nest of the white fishhawk up in the tree. Kongkong is the white fishhawk and his son is a smaller hawk called Min Kakalang.

See also *Cherbourg Aboriginal settlement; Flying foxes; Jirakupai; Murray river; Shields; Sky world; Southern Cross; Trade; Uluru; Wawilak sisters; Women ancestral beings.*

Spirit children Many *Aboriginal* groups believe that at certain strong places of the *earth*, or at certain *waterholes*, the spirits of children wait for a suitable womb in which to be born. A woman wishing to have a baby goes to these places to be entered by the spirit child. Often women know they are pregnant by the spirit child appearing to them in a dream; sometimes it is the male partner who has this dream. The dream and the particular fertility site determine the totem or *Dreaming* of the child.

To the *Tiwi people* of *Melville Island* spirit children are small dark-skinned people who have always existed. The Tiwis' beliefs are similar to those of other Aboriginal communities in that if one of these little people wishes to become a human being, he travels to a human camp and whispers to one of the married men while he is asleep, asking where his wife is. After the man has shown her to the spirit, it waits for a suitable opportunity to enter her body.

See also *Childbirth; Conception beliefs; Mopaditis; Mudungkala; Totems*.

Spirit snake Often during his initiation a shaman receives a spirit snake as his familiar which he uses to gather information and go into places where he cannot go as a person. The snake is connected to or itself forms the magic cord by which the shaman travels to the *sky world* where he or she may converse with the dead.

See also *Shamans*.

Stars and constellations All the stars and constellations have names and often are said to be ancestors who have ascended into the sky, with the twinkling stars being their campfires.

See *Aldebaran; Altair; Arcturus; Aurora Australis; Beehive; Bootes; Canis Major; Canopus; Capricornus; Centaurus; Coma Berenices; Cosmography; Delphinus; Dreaming tree of life; Formalhaut; Galaxy; Hydra; Mars; Milky Way; Mityan the moon; Moon; Morning Star; Orion; Pleiades; Rigel; Rober Carol; Sagittarius; Scorpio; Southern Cross; Tasmanian creation myth; Universe; Walkabout*.

Stevens, Thomas See *Arrernte landscape of Alice Springs*.

Sun In the duality of opposites that underlies much of *Aboriginal* belief, women are equated with light, life and wisdom, whereas men are equated with darkness, the shade, the night and *death*. So the sun is almost always considered to be female, and thus is connected with menstruation myths as well as light and warmth.

In the beginning the *Earth* was dark and beings had to find their way in the darkness with torches when seeking food and water. A *Koori* sun myth relates how a woman, Kyowee, left her small son sleeping in a cave while she went for *yams*. Without the sun there was little vegetation growing and she had to search long and hard. The ground was broken by gullies and ravines, and when she wished to return, she found that she was lost in the maze. She went on and on, until she reached the end of the world and stepped off the Earth and into the dark land above. Each day, she travels the vast plain, holding her torch above her head, looking for her son. It is her torch that lights up the whole world as she crosses the plain.

According to the *Tiwi people* of *Melville Island* the sun woman, Wuriupranala, received her role at the end of the *Dreamtime*. She travels daily across the sky with a torch of blazing bark, but before she sets out she powders her body with *red ochre*. When she reaches the end of her journey, she does this again, then rests for a time in the celestial lagoon, Kumpinulu, before returning to her home in the East along a subterranean valley.

See also *Cosmography; Eclipse of the sun; Emu; Gender roles; Universe; Yhi*.

Sydney See *Eora tribe; Kuringgai Chase National Park; Pemulwuy*.

T

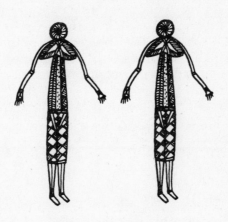

The Two Old Women

Taboo countries (or aversion countries) Some areas of Australia are taboo to the Australian *Aborigines*. One such is what is called 'the sickness country' in the Northern Territory, which was eventually mined for uranium; another is Wilson's Promontory, a peninsula jutting out into stormy Bass Strait. It was said to be presided over by the giant Lo-an and his wife Lo-an-tuka, who, according to the *Koori* Kulin people, became (respectively) the stars *Sirius* and star *Canopus*. Sometimes Lo-an descended from the sky onto a mountain peak which was sacred to him. If an unwary stranger entered the peninsula he would be attacked by the mysterious powers guarding it, so if a person wished to enter the land unharmed, he had to endure a number of rituals. First of all, he had to have all his hair shaved off. A streak of *red ochre* had to be painted down his chest and two white lines painted across his shoulders. He would then be fed on eels, once Lo-an's main food, then at dawn, if he heard the laughter of a kookaburra, he had to spit at the bird, for it was laughing at him for wishing to come into such a dangerous country. After the ceremony was over, he might venture onto the peninsula, at his own risk.

Tadjeri the brushtail possum See *Bunjil; Sagittarius.*

Taipan Taipan, the snake deity of the Wik Kalkan of *Cape York peninsula*, has all the attributes of such universal snake deities. He has the characteristics of a great primordial shaman and is considered the arbitrator of life and *death*. If he points a bone, the person dies; but he also can cure, for he controls the blood supply, the loss of which causes death. He is the deity who gave blood to humankind and who wields power over the physiological processes of men and women—the blood flow, the heart and menstruation. How Taipan provided the first blood supply is told in the following myth.

Once Taipan was a man and a great shaman. If a person was lying ill from swallowing the bones of goanna or bandicoot, he would make him well by squeezing him and sucking out the bone. Then he would expel it by spitting and the person would get well. However, at other times he would say, 'I can't cure you.' If he pointed a bone at a person, that person would soon die.

Taipan was very clever. He made thunder and *lightning*. He carried a big stone on the end of a long strong string and a blood-red knife. He would sharpen down a flint to a sharp point, fasten it to a long string and throw it. There would come a clap of thunder. He would throw it again and again thunder would come. The stone would become red hot, but would cool after a time.

Taipan had three wives: Uka (Water Snake), Mantya (Death-Adder) and Tuknampa, another water snake. He had one child, a son. This son was hunting downriver when he came across Tintauwa, a *black* water snake who was wife to Wala, the blue-tongued lizard. She seemed asleep, but was only pretending. Taipan's son came closer. She seduced him and they ran off together as sweethearts.

Wala followed the lovers and killed the son. He carried the heart and blood to Taipan, who became grief-stricken. Deciding to leave the *Earth*, he assembled his numerous family and, after rubbing the blood of his son on them, told them to descend into various places in the earth. He had two sisters and he gave them some blood and told them to carry it into the sky when they climbed up there. This is the red in the rainbow and symbolizes *menstrual blood.*

When he had done this, Taipan threw his blood-red knife and a storm arose. In it he disappeared into the earth. The two sisters pretended to go down into the earth, but instead rose again and climbed into the sky. In the dry season they stay under the ground, but when the stormy weather comes, they climb up into the sky with the elder brother of Taipan. The sisters are the red in the rainbow and the brother is the blue.

Now if a mother-in-law who has promised her daughter to a man holds her back, then Taipan throws his knife and thunder roars and lightning flashes and the quarrel is settled.

At Waityang, Tapipan's *djang* place, there is a milkwood tree next to the water. It is a place of great energy and if it is disturbed then many snakes gather there and a cyclonic wind rushes up to blow them away.

See also *Akurra serpent; Menstrual blood; Rainbow snake; Shamans*.

Tala places See *Thalu places*.

Talinini See *Pukamani funeral ceremonies*.

Tapalinga See *Universe*.

Tararalili See *Kulama ceremonies*.

Tarnung the gliding phalanger See *Sagittarius*.

Tasmania Tasmania is the large island below the south-eastern corner of the Australian continent. It was cut off from the mainland many thousands of years ago with the rising of the seas at the end of the last ice age. The island was inhabited by at least nine different groups divided into a number of clans. Most of the people were destroyed when the island was occupied by the British early in the nineteenth century and became a penal colony.

To all intents and purposes the Tasmanian *Aboriginal* cultures were destroyed when the few survivors were rounded up and exiled at Wybalenna on Flinders Island in Bass Strait. There they languished and many died whilst they were being 'civilized'. A handful of survivors were eventually returned to the larger island where they were placed in an institution at *Oyster Cove*. This place has now become a cultural centre and a *djang* site of endurance for the modern Tasmanian *Kooris*, who refuse to become absorbed into the majority Australian *community* and culture.

See also *Mutton bird; National Aboriginal Day; Relics of the dead; Tasmanian creation myth; Trugerninni*.

Tasmanian creation myth This creation myth was told by Wooraddi (died 1846), an elder and shaman of the Bruny Island *Aboriginal* people of *Tasmania*.

The two stars Moinee and Droemerdeener fought in the sky. Moinee was vanquished and exiled to the *Earth* where he died and became a large boulder off the coast at Sandy Bay. He made the first people, but failed to give them knees and they had tails like kangaroos. They had to stand all the time and Droemerdeener (*Canopus*) looked down and felt pity for them. He came down to Earth, cut off the tails and rubbed grease over the wounds. He added knees to the legs and at last the people felt they were complete.

See also *Creation myths*.

Tata the frog See *Flies*.

Terrania Creek basin and cave Terrania Creek basin in northern New South Wales in Bundjalung country and the cave there are said to have been an important spiritual area inhabited by many spirits. Even now people describe the basin as magical in atmosphere. The cave there is said to have been a *djang* site to the Widjabal clansmen of the Bundjalung. Young men in the last stages of initiation were taken there to gain strength and perseverance as well as to establish contact with the spirits. Much of the lore and history has not been revealed.

See also *Auwa; Bundjalung nation; Sacred places; Thalu places*.

Thalu places (or Tala places) are the strong places of the *Earth*. They are sacred places filled with energy or *djang*. Ceremonies performed at these sites are expected to keep up the numbers of the animal, plant, reptile, fish or plant or other thing(s) associated with the site, for example the proper ceremony performed by the custodian at the Rain Thalu should result in rain.

See also *Auwa; Djang; Sacred places; Walkabout*.

Thara the quail hawk See *Balayang; Bunjil; Crow*.

Thomas, Rover (Julama) (1926—) Rover Thomas is an artist from the *Kimberley* region of Western Australia who began painting in 1981. He comes from Warmun (Turkey Creek) and his work shows his deep spiritual affiliation with the land. He uses mainly ochres on a hardwood board.

See also *Palga*.

Thread cross See *Waningga*.

Thunder Man (Bodngo or Djambuwal) is an important ancestral
being of the *Duwa moiety* in *Arnhem Land*. In the *Dreamtime*, he lived
in the rain clouds. The Djanggawul saw him and sang about him on
their voyage from *Bralgu* to the mainland (see *Djanggawul and his
two sisters myth*). When he walks upon the waters, he causes huge
waves which are dangerous to *canoes*. He has a number of *sacred
places*, one of which he created when he threw his double-headed
club and broke the rocky face of a hill into fragments. The fragments are called his eyes and can still be seen in Arnhem Land.
When he threw the 'eyes' into the skies they formed clouds.

Thungutti See *Bundjalung nation*.

Tibrogargan See *Grasshouse mountains*.

Tiddalick the giant frog See *Echidna; Frog*.

Tide-lek See *Frog*.

Tintauwa See *Menstrual blood; Taipan*.

Tiwi people The Tiwi people are the inhabitants of *Melville Island*
and Bathurst Island off the northern coastline of Australia. They
are famous for their elaborate funeral services called the
Pukamani in which tall elaborate 'totem' poles are erected.
   See also *Bark paintings; Curlews; Cyclops; Mopaditis;
Mudungkala; Pukamani burial poles; Pukamani funeral ceremonies;
Spirit children; Sun; Tree between Heaven and Earth; Universe*.

Tjapaltjarri, Clifford Possum See *Papunya Tula art*.

Tjingal the emu See *Centaurus; Southern Cross*.

Tjukurrpa See *Dreamtime*.

Tjuringa *(churinga or tjurunga)* A *tjuringa* is a magic weapon and
sacred object, sometimes used as a *bull-roarer*. It is made of stone
or wood and is only to be shown to the men initiated into the

myths which it encodes. They are the only ones able to decipher the secret language engraved on them. *Tjuringas* are not only symbolic objects referring back to the *ancestral beings* or culture heroes, but are also said to be empowered with the energy flowing from them, hence their use as a magic weapon.

See also *Arrernte people; Djamar; Inma; Rangga*.

Tjurunga See *Tjuringa*.

Tnatantja poles *Tnatanja* poles are similar to totem poles and are used in the central and *Western Desert* in ceremonies. They are symbolic of the *Dreaming tree of life* and *death* and form a connection between heaven and *Earth*. In the *Dreamtime* the *tnatantja* pole was also employed as a magic weapon or implement, cleaving great gaps between rugged mountain ranges and carving out deep gullies. It is also regarded as a living creature, capable of independent action.

In the Dreamtime there was a great *tnatantja* pole at a place called Kerenbennga. It was long and slender, reached to the sky and was decorated with white and red down. Once a great wind arose. The pole bend under its onslaught. It struck the Earth and made a long narrow valley. It sprang upright again, but winds came from the north, south and west, finally blowing the pole down. It was later stolen and part of it became a bloodwood tree.

See also *Bandicoot ancestor*.

Toa sculptures (or Diyari sculptures) These interesting mythological icons seem to have marked a last creative spurt of the *Diyari people* before their culture collapsed. They are said to have developed under the influence of the German missionaries who set up a mission at Killalpaninna in Diyari country in 1866. It was at this mission that Toa sculptures were produced.

Today there are about 400 specimens in the South Australian museum and they have been divided into three types. The first group has a natural object attached to the head and may have painted designs on the stem and the head. The objects attached span the full range of physical objects available to the Diyari— pieces of vegetation, bird feathers, netting, stone tools, body parts, lizard feet, human hair, teeth and animal bones. They are said to symbolize the sacred *djang* places of the Diyari.

The second group of sculptures bears a carved or marked representation of either a man-made or natural object. The carved figures are of wood and the moulded ones are of gysum. The figures again range over Diyari life—*boomerangs*, body ornaments, bowls, geographical features, parts of human and animal bodies. On some the eyes and mouth are drawn in ochre.

The third type of Toa sculpture has the traditional wooden stem, but a gysum head painted with formal designs.

Toa are sad monuments to a culture which has not survived except in the papers of a few missionaries and anthropologists. It appears that the Diyari, conscious of the end of their beloved traditions and spirituality, encoded them in these sculptures which, unlike other sacred objects, are not secret but open to all, if only the key to decipher them could be found.

See also *Diyari people; Ground carvings and sculptures; Rock engravings*.

Tokumbimi Tokumbimi lived in the *Dreamtime* and ordered the ancestors to make sacred *djang* places on their old camp sites on *Melville Island* and Bathurst Island. He ordered them to make the food source for the people who were to come and then to change themselves into the particular bird, reptile, fish and other things with which the places were to be associated. He also made the laws which were to govern the people, how marriages were to be formed and also the kinship relations which were to order the people's lives. He also separated night from day. Later he changed himself into the yellow-faced honey-eater bird, *meliphaga chrysops*, and it is his call which awakens the *Tiwi people* to begin the day.

Tomituka See *Universe*.

Tookerrie the fish See *Narroondarie*.

Tooloom Falls (Dooloomi) Tooloom Falls in Bundjalung country in northern New South Wales is said to have come about because of the actions of Dirrangan. Dirrangan was an old woman who in the *Dreamtime* dammed the Clarence river and kept the water in a hidden spring. Balugaan, a handsome young man, enticed her to give him water. He noticed when he came to get the water that the secret spring was in reality a dam. He broke the dam and the waters gushed out, creating the Clarence river. Frantically, the old woman tried to recapture the water, building mountains, but the water flowed between them. She reached the mouth of the Clarence and became a stone pillar there.

See also *Bundjalung nation*.

Totems (or *Dreamings*) are one way of ordering the universe and the species therein. In the *Dreamtime* human beings were one with their Dreaming—humankind were *yams*, ants, owls, particular fish, waterlilies, turkeys, *emus*, wallabies, kangaroos and so on. Totem beings, the particular creative ancestors, often descended into the *earth* at particular places or energized particular places linked with a particular species. These *djang*, *thalu* or *wunggud* places are where those belonging to a particular totem or Dreaming go to activate the life force which ensures that a particular species continues on. Totem, or Dreaming, and person are intimately connected, and he or she has been given the task to continue the totemic species. It is the law passed down from the Dreamtime ancestors.

See also *Ancestral beings; Animal behaviour; Mopaditis; Spirit children; Tiwi people; Tnatantja poles; Trade; Wandjina*.

Totyerguil See *Altair; Capricornus; Corona Borealis; Murray river; Rigel*.

Trade Trade was very important to the *Aboriginal* people. This could be either the circulation of various objects between individuals belonging to different communities or regular trade fairs when many *tribes* came to barter goods.

The *Bibbulmum* people held *mana boming* or trade fairs at various centres during the year at which many items were exchanged, such as kangaroo skin bags, *spears* and *boomerangs*. One of these trade fairs was held in the Perth district. The Perth people had an ochre patch near Lake Monger and this was a stable trade item.

Trade was conducted over great distances, for example between the northern peoples and those of the south west, with goods passing from people to people until they reached their ultimate destination. When passing from tribe to tribe, trade items would be made up into bundles and all the articles would be marked with the totem mark of the sender or with ancestral designs. Items which might be in the bundle included *shields*, clapsticks, clubs, boomerangs, *hair string*, incised pearl shell pubic hair ornaments and ochres. These would be sent to men of the same kin or clan group, uncles, brothers or fathers. On receiving the goods, they would send back other items. If a tribe had enough, or more than enough, of any goods received, they would trade them on with other groups. There was thus a trading network, along which items from one tribe or country could pass for hundreds of kilometres.

See also *Pearl shell ornaments; Pituri; Red ochre*.

Tree between Heaven and Earth Trees or poles are important ceremonial and symbolic objects, ladders between the *Earth* and the *sky world*, the home of the ancestors, and between the dear departed and the living, thus in many communities corpses are placed in the branches of trees, in hollow trees or in specially prepared hollow logs placed upright in the ground. Logs such as these play an important part in funeral ceremonies such as the Pukamani poles amongst the Tiwi living on Bathurst and *Melville Islands*.

In certain ceremonies, *shamans* ascend such trees or poles to enter the sky world and the souls climb them to reach their final resting-place. Before being allowed to enter, the spirit or soul must pass a series of tests.

See also *Boomerang; Dreaming tree of life; Hollow log coffins; Matchwood tree; Pukamani burial poles; Pukamani funeral ceremonies; Tiwi people*.

Tribes The term 'tribe' was introduced into *Aboriginal* culture by the invaders. Although it is not really applicable to the *Aborigines* of Australia, it is now in general use among us. In the Australian Aboriginal context, tribe is reckoned by descent and tribal identity is locked into a number of local families who can trace their descent from a particular area and often from a particular ancestor or ancestors. These local groups speak a common language or dialect which is unique to them, or which has a pronunciation different from other groups, and at least the males of the group share a common ancestor or ancestors.

See also *Community; Kin groups; Kinship; Languages; Trade*.

Trickster character The trickster character, like Anansi of Jamaica and Coyote of the Native Americans, is also found in *Aboriginal* culture. He is sometimes a possum, othertimes *Crow*.

Paddy Roe, the story-teller and custodian of the *Dreaming track* in Broome, tells the story of the historical trickster character Mirdinan who killed his wife and turned into several animals, including a cat and an eaglehawk, to avoid capture. He was so powerful in his magic that no one could capture him. Eventually, his tricks were turned on him. He was made drunk, locked in a trunk and flung into the sea. It is interesting that he became an eaglehawk and not a crow. *Eaglehawk and Crow* stories are found all over Australia, and it usually is Crow who is the trickster and Eaglehawk the dupe, though often the tables are turned with the trickster being tricked.

There is a story from the *Murray river* in eastern Australia about

Mulyan the eaglehawk and Wahn the crow. One day Eaglehawk saw his wife talking to Magpie and became jealous. He beat her so severely that she died. The woman was Wahn's sister and it was his duty to avenge the murder. He came to Eaglehawk's camp and asked to rest awhile. He waited until Eaglehawk went out hunting and murdered his son as payback. To evade the consequences he made it appear that many men had taken part in the killing, but Eaglehawk was not taken in. He asked Crow to dig a deep grave for the dead child. Crow did so and when he descended into the pit with the body, Eaglehawk pushed all the *earth* on top of him and stamped it down. But Crow was also a great shaman, as tricksters are, and he escaped. He called up a great thunderstorm and a bolt of *lightning* hit the camp of Eaglehawk, wrecking it. This was in the *Dreamtime* when birds and animals were men, and just when Crow was exulting over his revenge, Mulyan rose in the shape of an eaglehawk and flew away. Crow did not escape completely either, for the lightning had scorched him, and when he became a bird to pursue Eaglehawk, he found that he was dark as night.

There are many stories of Aboriginal trickster spirits. Sometimes they are poltergeists, other times spirits who live in the rocks, crevasses of the earth and forest glades, or simply spirits of the Dreamtime.

There is a *Koori* myth about the Bullum-Boukan. These were two female spirits who were joined together and they had one son called Bullum-tut. One day the Bullum-Boukan smelt some women cooking fish and came to them and asked them for some. The women, knowing how mischievous they were, chased them away with their digging sticks. This upset the Bullum-Boukan and next day when the camp was deserted they went and scattered the *fires*, poured water on the ashes and carried off the live coals.

The people returned to find that their fire had been stolen. Ngarugal the musk crow tried to blow up the flames; he failed and went to Ngarang the swamp hawk for help. Ngarang flew off and found the Bullum-Boukan and their son far to the south on Wilson's Promontory, which juts out into the Southern Ocean. He swooped down and knocked some of the coals from them. This set fire to the grass. Bullum-Boukan stamped out the fire while their son, Bullum-tut, threw a cord made from *emu* sinews into the sky, where it stuck fast. He pulled at it and it broke. He tried another cord made from the sinews of a kangaroo and that too broke. He tried one made from the sinews of a red wallaby and it held fast. They began climbing up into the sky, but the hawk swooped and knocked more live coals from them. Tutbring the red-breasted robin held the burning coals to his chest and this is why he has a red breast.

Trugerninni (or Trugernanni, Truganini) (?–1876), along with her husband, Wooraddi, was one of the last *elders* of the *Tasmanian Koori* people and suffered the decimation and demise of her people and culture. Few of the myths of her people, the Bruny Islanders, still remain. When she died, her bones were placed on display in a museum and it was only after a long battle that they were finally given a sea burial. *National Aboriginal Day* is celebrated on the day of her *death*. This is done to stress the connection between the previous generations and the present.

See also *Oyster Cove; Tasmanian creation myth*.

Tukimbini See *Mudungkala; Pukamani funeral ceremonies*.

Tuknampa the water snake See *Taipan*.

Tukumbuna See *Mudungkala*.

Tul-Tul the plover See *Quinkin*.

Tundun See *All-Fathers; Aurora Australis*.

Tuniruna See *Universe*.

Tupatupini the small owl See *Kulama ceremonies*.

Turnong the glider possum See *Bunjil*.

Tutbring the red-breasted robin See *Trickster character*.

Tuurap Warneen Tuurap Warneen was one of the last great *shamans* of the *Koori* people of Victoria. He lived in the latter part of the nineteenth century and was finally murdered by an invader.

Once when doubts were expressed at his ability to fly above the clouds and bring back one of the spirits called Wirtin Wirtin Jaawan, he flew into the air and brought one back in the shape of an old woman wrapped in a possum-skin rug and tied around the waist with a rope. He explained that the spirit had to be kept tied up as it might injure people. After half an hour, he led her off.

Two Brothers (the Bram-Bram-Bult) The Two Brothers, Yuree and Wanjel (Castor and Pollux), are the ancestral heroes of a huge corpus of myths which stretched across Victoria. Essentially, they belonged to the Wotjobaluk *Koori* people, but, like the other great mythic cycles which stretch for many hundreds, if not thousands, of kilometres, they extend beyond tribal boundaries.

The myth cycle is set in the *Dreamtime* when Purra the kangaroo was bounding along in his efforts to escape from Doan the glider possum, who was chasing him. Doan had almost caught Purra when he came to the country of Wembulin the triantelope, who was camped with his two daughters. Wembulin attacked Doan, who first managed to escape, but then Wembulin came after him and caught and ate him.

Next Wembulin and his two daughters went after Purra. Doan's maternal uncles, the Bram-Bram-Bult, followed after him to see what was happening. They met Mara the sugar ant, who was carrying a hair of Doan, then several of Mara's sisters and brothers who were carrying scraps of Doan's skin and body back to their camp. They came to the place where Wembulin had attacked Doan and in the attack had sheared through trees. They came upon Doan's bones and knew that he had been killed and eaten. Out for revenge, they followed Wembulin. They passed two of his old camp sites and at the third found his two daughters busily pounding honeysuckle seeds into flour for cakes. Wembulin was in a bark shelter and the brothers laid an ambush, then killed him. They took his daughters for wives and began their return journey, but on the way they killed the two women because they were afraid of their savage nature.

The next adventure the brothers had was with Jinijinitch the great white owl and his two sons who were cannibals and so bloodthirsty that they had killed their mother and wife for food. The two brothers were also great *shamans* and they sang up a storm. Great White Owl and his sons went into their bark hut to escape the storm and the two brothers set *fire* to it and burnt them up.

The ancestral brothers had many adventures as they wandered over the land, taming and naming it. Eventually the younger brother was injured in a fight with Gertuk the mopoke and a snake bit him and he died, in spite of the elder brother's nursing. The elder Bram-Bram-Bult was so overcome with grief that he fashioned a manikin from the trunk of a tree, magically imbued it with life and ordered it to become his brother. They then journeyed to the west where it is said that they lived in a cave for a long time.

Now they have ascended into the *sky world*, where they may be seen as the two stars in the forelegs of *Centaurus*, the pointers to the *Southern Cross*. Their mother, Druk the *frog*, is with them. She is the star in the Southern Cross nearest to the pointers.

See also *Beehive*.

Two Men myth The Two Men (*Wati Gudjara*) myth involves a long and arduous journey by two iguana men, the elder brother Kurukadi and the younger Mumba, who travel south east from the *Kimberley* to imprint their deeds and adventures not only upon the landscape, but upon the local ancestral spirits. They are said to have had a magic *boomerang* with which they fashioned much of the landscape of the *Western Desert*. Ancestral cultural heroes, they initiated songs and *dances* and passed on sacred designs and images which are still being used today.

The Two Men myth may be seen as a connecting myth, in that it connects the ancestral spirits through interaction and relationship along a route extending for thousands of kilometres. I have had stories related to me in the Kimberley, but have never found the beginnings of their journey. The journey continues into South Australia, Pitjantjatjara country, where at long last it is said the two men ascended into the skies. The length of the journey is echoed in the myth of the seven sisters who also came from the West and eventually ascended into the sky to become the *Pleiades*.

The Two Men myth is an example of how a myth may extend over tribal boundaries and cultures. The *Wati Gudjara* covered thousands of kilometres before they left the *Earth* to become two stars in Gemini.

See also *Inma boards; Two Old Women; Waningga*.

Two Old Women The myth of the Two Old Women—'old' being used in an honorary sense as a mark of respect rather than description of age—is narrated by the *elders* of the *Adnyamathanha people*. They are said to be the wives of the two mates, who appear to be a continuation of the *Two Men myth*, or a local variant of it. The two mates ascended into the sky leaving the two old women alone. They tracked the men to a place called Wakarra Virrinha and saw two long stones lying on the ground which are said to be the two men, but the women continued tracking and had various adventures.

Eventually one of the women fell down a cliff and burst into a hundred pieces. Where the pieces landed, grass trees sprang up and today there are more grass trees at this place than anywhere else. The remaining woman continued her travels and disappeared into the neighbouring territory of the Arabana people.

See also *Women ancestral beings*.

Tyit the fish hawk See *Mbu the ghost*.

U

Uluru—Ayer's Rock

Uka the water snake See *Taipan*.

Uluru Uluru is a telluric or *djang* place of amazing potency and it
is perhaps the only place of pilgrimage in Australia visited by
people of all races and nationalities. People go there for a mystical
experience and many do achieve it. It is a place of male and female
sacred places, quiet caves and pools, and phallic upthrustings of
rock, and in the distance lies *Katatjuta*, also a sacred energy place.

Uluru is perhaps the most sacred place for *Aboriginal* people
right across Australia, for here the many *song lines* and *Dreaming
tracks* come together in a unity of myth which is celebrated by the
giant sandstone monolith rising nearly 400 metres above the surrounding countryside. The monolith was built in the *Tjukurrpa* or
Dreamtime by two boys who played in the mud after rain. When
they had finished they travelled south to Wiputa, on the northern
side of the Musgrave Range, where they killed and cooked a euro,
then turned north again and made their way to table-topped
Mount Connor, where their bodies are seen today as boulders.

The custodianship of Uluru is with the Pitjantjatjara and
Yankuntjatjara people and ownership has been inherited from
both mothers' and fathers' sides. The rock itself is divided into the
sunny side and the shady side, which not only refers to genera-
tional divisions but also to the division between two great myth
cycles whose central themes motivate most of central Australian
Aboriginal society, much as the great myths found in the
Mahabharata motivates much of Hindu society. Opposites meet
here in an uneasy tension which was resolved in a great battle
which marks the end of the Dreamtime age and the beginning of
our own age.

The mythology of the 'shade' concerns the Kuniya, the Rock
Python people. They came in three groups to Uluru, from the
west, south and north. One of the Kuniya carried her eggs on her
head, using a *manguri* (grass-head pad) to cushion them. She
buried these eggs at the eastern end of Uluru. When I was at
Uluru a few years ago I watched a woman performing what has
become an age-old ritual at the base of the rock. In the *dance* her
feet dragged in the sand, leaving the tracks of a snake.

While they were camped at Uluru the Kuniya were attacked by
a party of Liru, poisonous snake warriors. At Alyurungu, on the
south-west face of the rock, are pock marks, the scars left by the
warriors' *spears*, and two *black*-stained watercourses there are
the transformed bodies of two Liru warriors. When it rains the
water channels down these watercourses but often they are dry
and thus only marks.

The battle centred on Mutjitjulu, a section of the north-eastern
part of the rock. There is an Aboriginal settlement there. Here a
Kuniya woman fought with her digging stick and her features are
preserved on the eastern face of the gorge, while the features of
the attacking Liru warrior can be seen on the western face, where
his eyes, head wounds (transformed into vertical cracks) and sev-
ered nose form part of the cliff. Above Mutjitjulu is Uluru rock
hole. This is the home of a Kuniya who releases water into
Mutjitjulu.

The Liru had been called down upon the Kuniya by the Mulga
Seed men, for they had also refused the Mulga Seed men's invitation to their ceremonies. They too were defeated and retreated to
the east.

There are also stories of other ancestors who entered into this
vast battle, a veritable battle of the scale which occurs in the
Indian epic the *Mahabharata* and signals the end of an era, the
creative period of the *Dreamtime*.

See also *Great battles; Pungalunga men; Yugumbir people.*

Umpampurru See *Pea Hill*.

Underworld As there is a belief in a *sky world* among many *Aboriginal tribes*, so there is also a belief in an underworld.

From the *Murray river* people comes a myth about a magpie who was digging a hole to find food. He dug deeper and deeper and suddenly fell through the bottom of the hole. When he looked around, he found himself in another world. There were trees about. Then he heard a pecking noise. He went in the direction of the noise and found a cockatoo digging grubs out of a tree. The cockatoo sang a song of welcome to him, then asked him if he was happy living in that world. Magpie said that he preferred his own up above, so Cockatoo invited him to get on his back. He flew up to the ceiling of the underworld, found the hole and flew through. He left Magpie there and returned to the underworld.

See also *Cosmography; Sky world; Universe*.

Ungarr See *Quinkin*.

Uniapon, David (1862–1967) David Uniapon belonged to the *Nanga* people of South Australia. He was born in Port McLeay in South Australia. He is an important historical figure who attempted a synthesis of *Aboriginal* and Christian beliefs. The beginnings of the modern Aboriginal cult of *Biame* (which is a synthesis of Aboriginal and Christian beliefs) may be traced back to him. Some of his important mythological stories are found in the anthology of Aboriginal writings, *Paperbark*.

See also *Narroondarie*.

Universe The universe for the *Tiwi people* consists of four levels: (a) the *underworld*, Ilara; (b) the *Earth*; (c), the *sky world*, Juwuku; and (d) a further sky world, Tuniruna.

Ilara is said to be always dark and there are two high stony ridges with a valley between. It is along this valley that the *sun*-woman and the *moon*-man travel each day from the western horizon to their homes in the east. No food can be found in the underworld, but a stream flows from one of the mountain ridges.

The sky world, according to the Tiwi, is where during the *monsoon*, Pakadringa, the man of the thunderstorms; Tomituka, the woman of the monsoonal rains and Bumerali, the *lightning* woman with her many children make their homes. Across it travel the sun-woman, the moon-man, the men of the *Milky Way* and various star-women.

Above the sky world is the world Tuniruna, which is the daytime home of numerous star-women, the Tapalinga, and the men of the Milky Way, the Maludaianiniu. During the dry season, the beings associated with the monsoon make their homes here.

See also *Cosmography; Galaxy; Stars and constellations*.

Unurgunite See *Canis Major; Mityan the moon*.

Unyupu See *Pea Hill*.

Urdlu See *Flinders Range*.

Urngi See *Shamans*.

Utemorrah, Daisy (1922–94) Daisy Utemorrah was an elder of the *Ngarinjin* people and lived at Mowanjum just outside Derby in the *Kimberley* region of Western Australia. She was active in spreading knowledge of her culture and had a number of her stories published. I met her and *David Mowaljarlai* in Fitzroy Crossing at a language meeting and listened to her stories detailing the long-ago exploits of her ancestors, the *Wandjina*. She died when this book was being compiled and her *death* is a sad loss to us all. She was a very dynamic woman, best known for her book *Do Not Go Around the Edges*.

See also *Great flood*.

W

Wandjina ancestor

Waa See *Canopus; Crow; Rober Carol.*

Wagyal (or Waugal; Woggal) The Wagyal is an important ancestral deity, or deities, of the *Nyungar* country of south-western Australia. It is one and many, male and female, and resides in *waterholes* and rivers. If disturbed, it is said the Wagyal will bring catastrophe on our people.

The Wagyal watches over the food and other laws, and punishes those who transgress them. It may be likened to a dragon, for the one in the former *Minjelungin* swamp, now the Perth suburb of Swan Districts, had hair on its back and flap-like wings.

in the *Dreamtime* the Wagyal travelled through the south west, leaving traces of its journey at certain places. It made all the big rivers and the tracks of its journey, the *Dreaming tracks* and *song lines*, link up with other snake sites throughout Australia.

See also *Akurra serpent; Ancestral beings; Bennett's Brook; Dreaming; Rainbow snake; Yagan.*

Waia See *Mudungkala*.

Waityang See *Taipan*.

Waiyauwa See *Dilly bags*.

Waka See *Crocodiles*.

Waka Waki people See *Cherbourg Aboriginal settlement*.

Wakarla See *Eagle*.

Walanggar the death adder See *Great corroborees*.

Walbiri creation myth Creation for the Walbiri people occurred at the *Winbaraku* sacred complex. The world of living things and shapes became manifest through the workings of Mamu-boijunda the great spider and *Jarapiri* the great snake who emerged from the *earth* at Winbaraku. Jealousy (*fire*) and desire came with them and this resulted in the first ancestors leaving their home behind to travel across the land while the giant spider retreated to a cave deep beneath the hill.
    See also *Ancestral beings; Creation myths*.

Walbiri people See *Dogs; Jarapiri; Yuendumu*.

Walguna See *Wullunggnari*.

Walkabout is a word which has been coined to describe the pilgrimages that *Aboriginal* people must make to their *sacred places* to conduct ceremonies. Often it is used in a derogatory fashion, meaning just aimless wandering. *Aborigines* have never been aimless wanderers, but have always followed well-defined paths across their land. They have done so for thousands upon thousands of years and continue to do so when conditions permit, enacting the great journeys, or sections of them, that the *ancestral beings* undertook long ago in the *Dreamtime*.
    Walkabout is seen to reflect the circulation of the planets about the *sun*, and the rise and fall of the stars. In fact, it was the stars and their positions in the sky which determined many aspects of

the lives of the Aborigines, including the direction of pilgrimage. As all the universe was in motion, so were the Aboriginal people.

See also *Cosmography; Djang; Dreaming tracks; Song lines; Stars and constellations; Thalu places*.

Walmajarri people See *Walmatjarri people*.

Walmatjarri people (or Walmajarri) The Walmatjarri people are a desert people who migrated to the *Kimberley* region in the middle decades of this century. They originally lived in the Great Sandy Desert, which consists of long rolling sandhills or ridges with flat country between them. The Walmatjarri were nomadic, travelling in small family bands from waterhole to waterhole. In some *waterholes* lived water snakes with whiskers, legs and scaly dorsal spines. They were remarkably like dragons. If they smelt that approaching people were strangers, they could be dangerous. Because of the importance of water to the Walmatjarri, many of their religious beliefs were based on it, as the provider of life, and they believed that all the waterholes were linked up by underground passages along which the water snakes could travel.

See also *Community; Pike, Jimmy; Skipper, Peter*.

Walpa Gorge See *Katatjuta*.

Wanambi See *Katatjuta*.

Wandjina The Wandjina are the spirit ancestors of the *Kimberley*. The *Aboriginal* people of the Kimberley believe that the Wandjina created the world and walked about in human form, making places and naming animals and plants. They left their images on the walls of caves, images of *earth* potency.

It was in the Lalai, the beginning, the *Dreamtime*, that the Wandjina appeared from the sky, with their heads surrounded by circles of *lightning* and thunder, and dressed in a curtain of rain. Thus they are connected with the sky, water and rain.

Each Wandjina has his own name and there is always a male custodian who claims him as his mother's brother—the most important relationship. The custodianship is usually passed down from father to a person in a son relationship, especially to one who has felt a spiritual relationship to the particular Wandjina which inhabits the site.

Along with the cave images of the Wandjina are also images of the *totems* or *Dreaming*s of that particular group of people. All

Wandjina sites are *wunggud*, places of concentrated earth power
and life-force which is kept radiating by retouching the images, or
merely by visiting the sacred power site and singing the songs
associated with it.

See also *Ancestral beings; Great flood; Ngarinjin; Palga;
Utemorrah, Daisy; Wullunggnari.*

Wangal See *Gulibunjay and his magic boomerang.*

Wangarr Wangarr are the ancestral spirit beings of the Yolngu
people of *Arnhem Land.*

See also *Morning Star; Rom ceremony of Arnhem Land.*

Waningga The *waningga* (or thread cross) is a sacred object made
by tying two sticks into a cross, or three sticks into a double cross,
and then stringing parallel bands of *hair string* across the resulting
frame. *Waningga* are used all across the *Western Desert* and one was
made by the ancestral heroes, the *Two Men, Wati Gutjara*. They
vary in size from small hair string crosses which could be stuck into
the hair of the performers of a ritual to much larger ones which
were carried on the shoulders or stuck into the ground. They are
said to represent the sacred *djang* sites and can hold some of the
energy of the site.

Wanjel See *Beehive.*

Wanungamulangwa people See *Dolphins.*

Warka See *Crocodiles.*

Warmalana (Depuch Island) Warmalana Island was formed in
the *Dreaming* by Maralga, one of a group of spirit men who play a
leading role in the Pilbara. They can be recognized in carvings by
their long penises which symbolize their importance in initiation
rites. Maralga created the island by lifting up a huge rock, carrying it on his head down to the seashore and flinging it into the sea.

As is shown by the story, this island became a great *djang* place.
It lies just off the coast and south of Port Hedland. Its rocks and
boulders are covered with an immense number of carved figures
detailing the lives of the local *Aboriginal* people and their beliefs
over millennia. Now it is all but deserted and the intense ritual life
is all but gone. Only the engraved figures testify to its importance.

Warnampi Kutjara See *Western Desert.*

Warramurrungundji Warramurrungundji the All-Mother's myth and travels are related by *Bill Neidjie* in his book *Story about Feeling.* She was a *rainbow snake* who came from the sea and travelled across the land, making the law and forming part of the landscape of *Kakadu National Park.* Her travels came to an end when she saw the first flash of *lightning* and felt shame. She turned into a rock which may still be seen today. She is thought to bring the *monsoon* rains to the Northern Territory.

See also *All-Mothers.*

Warta Vurdli See *Morning Star.*

Water sprites (*Burrawungal*) Water sprites, usually female, are thought to live in some pools by many *Aboriginal* people. They can be dangerous to the unwary, for it is said that they lie waiting to trap unwary males who might venture into the water, dragging them down and drowning them.

A story is told by the *Yarrabah* people about a man who went hunting eels. He went along a watercourse and saw two women. He sneaked up on them and grasped the younger, after first rubbing sand on his hands, as she was a *burrawungal*, a water sprite, and thus very slippery. He took her back to camp and warmed her all over so that the slime on her skin disappeared. He made her his wife and told everyone not to let her go near the river. But one day, she managed to slip away, disappeared into the water and was never seen again.

See also *Waterholes.*

Waterholes Waterholes are often considered sacred as they are the habitats of giant water snakes. The *Ngarinjin* elder *David Mowaljarlai* says about one such waterhole in his country, 'Never go into Wunggud water because this waterhole is where Wunggud decided to stop. We dream children from this Wunggud, and in the Wunggud water we swim when we are sick. The power cleanses us from that sickness.'

See also *Altair; Bandicoot ancestor; Bunyip; Crocodiles; Flying foxes; Katatjuta; Kulunbar; Millstream pools; Murray river; Spirit children; Water sprites; Wagyal; Walmatjarri people; Wawilak sisters.*

Watharung See *Melbourne.*

Wati Gudjara See *Two Men myth*.

Waugal See *Wagyal*.

Wawilag sisters See *Wawilak sisters*.

Wawilak sisters (or Wawilag sisters) The two Wawilak sisters are
the centre of a corpus of myths in *Arnhem Land*. It is said that they
arrived at Trial Bay in the south-east of Arnhem Land went on to
the Arafura Sea. The younger sister was pregnant and the older sister already had a baby which she carried in a paperbark cradle.
They both carried *spears* and killed goannas, possums and bandicoots for food as well as gathering plant food. They named the
plants as they travelled along.

Suddenly the younger sister felt the contractions of birth beginning. They made camp at the edge of the great Mirarrmina waterhole beneath the waters of which lived the giant snake *Yulunggul*.
They began cooking food, but as they placed the food on the *fire*,
each type jumped up and into the pool. This was because it all
belonged to the owner of the country, Yulunggul.

The elder sister went into the pool. She was menstruating and
this alerted the giant snake. He came out of his lair and saw the
two sisters. Angrily he hissed and *lightning* flashed. He rose on his
tail and his head touched the sky. The elder sister began dancing
and chanting to control him, but he swallowed the younger sister
and her baby. The elder sister fled in terror and was eventually
eaten by leeches.

Different communities have their own versions of the myth and
variations occur. In oral storytelling, the narrator, while sticking to
the main line of the myth, often leaves out details, especially of a
secret nature, depending on the composition of the audience.

Later Yulunggul lifted up his head and spoke to other giant
snakes of the *Duwa moiety* from other areas of *north-eastern Arnhem
Land* about their different dialects and food. At first he denied
that he had eaten the younger sister and her baby, but later he
admitted this. When he did so the south-east *monsoon* began to
come in, and he roared and fell to the ground. He split open the
ground and made a river, then he vomited up the sister and her
child. He dropped them on an ants' nest, then crawled back to his
waterhole. The ants bit the younger sister and the baby and they
came to life again.

This is only an extremely short version of the myth, and a single
version. There are other versions which differ in details, but what
is important is the connection between the arrival of the monsoon

blowing from Asia and the Wawilak sisters, their differing customs, such as the carrying of spears, and the antagonism caused by their upsetting the giant chthonic snake Yulunggul.

The Wawilak sisters corpus of myths forms the basis of the *Gunabibi ceremonies*.

See also *Bark paintings; Gunabibi; Woijal*.

Weet-kurrk See *Arcturus; Bootes*.

Weeun See *Shamans*.

Wellington Rocks See *Woollool Woollool*.

Wembulin the triantelope See *Two Brothers*.

Western Desert The Western Desert, because of its inhospitability to the invaders, is still filled with the richness of traditional *Aboriginal* culture, though the area, with its living traditions, is under threat by mining companies who refuse to accept that there is such a thing as the sacred.

In the *Tjukurrpa*, the *Dreamtime*, many ancestors travelled across the land. There were the *Two Men*, or *Wati Gudjara*, who in this tradition are said to have come up from my country, the south west, after they piled up the rocks and mud to make the coastline. Then there are the *Kungkarangkalpa*, the seven sisters who eventually became the *Pleiades*; the *Warnampi Kutjara*, the two water snakes, and then the *Minyma Kutjara*, the *Two Old Women* who travelled far east and north and south to the *Flinders Range*. All of these *ancestral beings* left their signs all across the desert landscape. Their presence is always felt and remembered and recreated in the stories and ceremonies, *dances* and songs which actualize the ever-present sacred and unite it with our everyday lives.

See also *Djang; Dogs; Inma boards; Languages; Papunya; Papunya Tula art; Tnatantja poles; Waningga; Women ancestral beings; Yuendumu*.

White Lady White Lady was a famous *Koori* shaman of the nineteenth century. Her power was said to emanate from a long *red ochre* painted staff. For some healing ceremonies she decorated it with white cockatoo feathers. On moonlit nights she left the camp with an empty bag and returned with it filled with snakes. On one occasion she made a shamanistic journey to the *moon* and returned with the tail of what she called a 'lunar kangaroo'.

See also *Shamans*.

White ochre (or pipeclay) There is a myth that white ochre was first used by the giant kangaroo ancestors who passed its use on to humankind during the *Dreaming*. It is a sacred colour of the *Duwa moiety*.

See also *Bark paintings; Flying foxes; Frog; Great battles; Morning Star; Red, black, yellow and white; Red ochre; Yellow ochre*.

Widjabal See *Bundjalung nation; Terrania Creek basin and cave*.

Wik Kalkan See *Wik Munggan*.

Wik Munggan Wik Munggan is the collective name given to a number of clans inhabiting the western coast of *Cape York peninsula*. Some of the names of the clans are: Tyongandyi, Yupngati, Ndraangit, Kalkan and Kandyu. The Wik Munggan people were collected together onto missions and reserves such as Mapoon, Weipa and Arakun, where their culture was modified under the influence of missionaries and government agents.

See also *Auwa; Bark huts and shelters; Cape York peninsula; Childbirth; Dilly bags; Fire; First man child; First woman; Flies; Flying foxes; Mangrove woman; Menstrual blood; Moipaka; Moiya and paka-paka; Oyster and Shark; Seagull and Torres Strait Pigeon; Spears; Yams*.

Wildu See *Eagle*.

Wilindu See *Mudungkala*.

Willy wagtail (Jitta Jitta) In our *Bibbulmum* culture, the willy wagtail is a gossip bird or messenger bird. He comes hopping about and tells us all the news of our relatives. He should always be greeted and fed. He is also the protector of the camp and must be treated with respect.

There is a story about Jitta Jitta that has been handed down to us as a warning. In the old days our mothers and fathers used to go out and leave the children under the protection of Jitta Jitta. He used to look after them, but no one paid him for his services. No one ever paid him anything, so one day he dug a hole in the riverbank, made it into a house and put the children inside. He lit a *fire* above the hole and the smoke of the fire suffocated them all. He then put out the campfires, took a firestick and carried it to the sea. He was about to put it into the sea when the hawk came flying and saw what he was doing. He snatched the firestick away, because it was the first and only fire in the world then. He took the fire back to the camp and told the people that they should respect Jitta Jitta or else he would always cause trouble. If he was respected, however, he would always befriend the people. We made our peace with Jitta Jitta and now he is our protector.

See also *Eagle; Peewit; Yugumbir people.*

Wiltja See Red ochre.

Wilunduela See *Mudungkala.*

Winbaraku Winbaraku is a *sacred place* in the Ngalia country, west of Haast's Bluff in the Macdonnell Range, central Australia. It is the birthplace of the great snake *Jarapiri*, a creative ancestor who made the *earth*.

Winbaraku consists of two main peaks, the taller of which is the great snake and the lesser, abutting his own, are the Nabanunga women who came to take him to their camp. He, however, coiled himself on the ground and refused to move.

There are many *Dreaming* ancestors connected to the site: Hare-Wallaby, Jukulpa and the important Melatji *dogs*; Mamu-boijunda the barking spider and another snake, Jarapiri Bomba, who is also equated with the lesser peak. The sacred complex is under the custodianship of Walbiri *elders.* Important *Aboriginal* sites are usually connected to more than one ancestor. Many ancestors on their travels come there and interrelate. Thus the sites often belong to more than one clan.

Wirnum is the *Koori* word for clever man, native doctor, shaman or medicine man in the south-eastern region. These were the men who controlled the initiation ceremonies in the *boro circles.*

See also *Initiation process; Shamans.*

Wirtin Wirtin Jaawan See *Tuurap Warneen.*

Wodoi See *Kimberley.*

Woggal See *Wagyal*.

Woijal Woijal, the wild *honey* ancestor, lived in the *Dreamtime* and in the same country as the *Wawilak sisters* and his myth is closely interwoven with theirs.

Woijal set out from Ngalagan country travelling northwards, carrying his *spears*, a spear thrower and a sonte axe. When he came across bees hiving in trees, he cut them down and filled his long bags, which he carried over his shoulders, with honeycomb. When he cut the trees and they fell to the ground, they created rivers. Woijal created a number of *djang* places.

Wolkolan See *Mangrove woman*.

Wollumbin (Mount Warning) is the remains of a volcano which dominates the Tweed Valley on the borders of New South Wales and Queensland. It was a very sacred initiation site, once marked with a monument of stones beyond which only fully initiated men could go.

Wollumbin means 'warrior' and it is said that the scars on the mountainside are the initiation marks of the warrior. From certain angles, the face of the mountain resolves itself into the face of the *Aboriginal* warrior.

See also *Initiation process*.

Women ancestral beings Myths of women *ancestral beings* are found all across Australia. The beings engage in long journeys, creating the landscape and naming the fauna and flora. For example in the *Western Desert*, just as there is the *Two Men myth*, so there is the *Two Old Women* myth, which details the journey of two ancestral women who move south from the central desert to the southern ocean and back again.

As they travelled, the two women made many natural features, which today are repositories, endowed with the women's spiritual essences and energies.

In adjacent areas, they are called the *Kurinpi* women and are two knowledgeable and respected women who travel across the country naming it and performing ceremonies. It is said that they taught men to throw *spears* overarm and also gave (or had stolen from them by men) the ritual objects and ceremonial designs they carried with them. This theme of men stealing or getting from ancestral women ceremonies and ceremonial objects is found in many myths in which women feature as the main characters (see also *Fire*).

Woodbarl the white cloud See *Giant dogs*.

Woollool Woollool (Wellington Rocks) Woollool Woollool, in Bundjalung country, northern New South Wales, rises to a height of 1,040 metres above sea level. It is bounded on all sides by the Cataract river and its tributaries draining north into the Clarence river. It is the home of the Woollool Woollool spirit who travels around the mountains and down to the coast. It is an important place for *shamans*, who make their magic here. Only shamans can go to the place and people who approach it are warned off by the Woollool Woollool spirit. The site may, however, be viewed from a distance.
See also *Bundjalung nation*.

Woomera The woomera is a spear thrower, an instrument which gives the spear added impetus when thrown.
See also *Barrier Reef*.

Woonamurra, Banjo Banjo Woonamurra lives in Derby in the *Kimberley* region of Western Australia. He is a story-teller and custodian of the lore of his *Bunuba people*. He is considered to be an important 'owner' of the story of *Jandamara*, or Pigeon, an important *Aboriginal* resistance fighter of the late nineteenth century.

Wooraddi See *Tasmanian creation myth; Trugernanni*.

Worora See *Creation myths; Kimberley; Ngarinjin*.

Wotjobaluk See *Antares; Canis Major; Galaxy; Koori; Magellan Clouds; New moon; Rigel; Two Brothers*.

Wudu ceremony of the Kimberley The Wudu ceremony was an educational practice which was repeated daily. A close-relative's *fire*-purified hand was passed over the body of the young child being educated. As each part was touched, an instruction was given, such as, for the lips, 'Do not speak bad things, always speak true.'
See also *Kimberley*.

Wuka See *Flying foxes*.

Wullunggnari on the Mitchell plateau, *Kimberley*, is a very sacred place of the Kimberley people where three stones represent the *great flood*. It is where a *Wandjina* came to take his final rest. At the place is a stone altar before a cave and beneath stands *Walguna*, the Tree of Wisdom, Knowledge and Law. At times of ceremony, this tree is hung with sacred objects.

Here, *David Mowaljarlai* states, men and women would gather to be reborn of water and spirit. They would come to the site completely naked without weapons and tools. The priests, those long initiated in the ceremony, prepared the initiates for a week with teachings about the site and ceremony. Sacrifices were made and small pieces of meat, the flesh of the Wandjina, were taken. Men and women were then bathed in sacred wunggud waters at different places according to gender. As a final ritual, they passed through the raised arms of two elders, then jumped through purifying mushroom smoke.

See also *Initiation process; Sacred places; Thalju places*.

Wuriupranala See *Mudungkala; Sun*.

Wuriuprinili See *Mudungkala*.

Wurundjeri See *Melbourne; Yarra river and Port Phillip*.

Wybalenna on Flinders Island in Bass Strait is the place where the remnants of the Tasmania *Aboriginal* people were exiled. Many died there.

See also *Oyster Cove; Tasmania*.

Y

Yulunggul, the giant serpent

Yaburara people See *Burrup peninsula*.

Yagan Yagan is an important ancestor of the *Nyungar* people. When *Bibbulmum* country was invaded in 1829, he and the rest of his people saw the invaders as the spirits of the dead returning. This belief lasted for a time, but then conflict arose when the Bibbulmum found out that the so-called 'spirits' had come to take their land. The newcomers did not respect tribal law or traditions, though expecting that their own laws be obeyed by the Bibbulmum.

Conflict began. Yagan led a resistance movement and was captured. He was transported to a tiny island off the coast, but managed to escape. Then a year later, his brother, Domjum, was shot dead. In retaliation, Yagan and his father, Midgegooroo, began again their war of resistance against the cruel invaders. They were declared 'outlaws' and a reward was set on their heads. Midgegooroo was caught and executed. Yagan evaded capture for three months, then was shot dead in an ambush.

Yagan's *death* hastened the end of resistance around the invaders' main settlement at Perth on the Swan river, next to a sacred site of the *Wagyal*. It was not long after that they cleared the area with a wholesale massacre of men, women and children at Pinjarra. With this massacre, organized resistance against the British came to an end.

It is said that the red sap of the bloodwood tree is the blood Yagan shed in defence of his land and people.

Ya-itma-thang See *Koori*.

Yamadji The Yamadji people live above *Bibbulmum* country in the coastal areas above the town of Geraldton and below the *Kimberley* region.

Yams Yams are a very important food source to the Australian *Aborigines* and the gathering and preparing of them for food is a woman's occupation. It is thus only natural that the yam is seen as a woman and often is part of women's 'business'.

In *Cape York peninsula*, there are two types of yams: the soft yam and the hard yam. The soft yam is cooked in the ashes of a fire. The hard yam is sour to the taste and needs quite a bit of preparation. It is cooked in an ant-bed oven, then crushed and washed in water, sieved through the meshes of a dilly bag, then left to dry in a bark vessel.

The *Wik Munggan* people narrate many myths about the yam. There is one story about the hard yam. In the *Dreamtime*, the hard yam was going about as a woman. She lived upstream and downstream lived the edible plant Arrowroot, who was a man. Once she came downstream to get a bailer shell to use in rinsing food and the arrowroot man barred her way. They quarrelled, made up and began living as man and wife, but they always quarrelled. They separated and the woman spent her time gathering and preparing yams (as in these myths, the way of preparing yams and other root foods is described).

Then one day the hard yam woman finds that she is lame. She becomes sick and can only crawl. She digs a hole and sits in it. It is too shallow and she digs some more. The *sun* shines and it is hot. She needs water and she feels that she must get out of the hole, grow to the top of her hole to get it, but the sides of the hole are too steep and she can't get out. She sinks further into the *earth*, saying, 'Just in this way, the yam will sit in its hole and my place will become the yam *djang* place. From here yams will go out in plenty to women for food.'

See also *Childbirth; Crow; Kulama ceremonies; Sun; Totems.*

Yamuti See *Extinct giant marsupials.*

Yar Birrain See *Bundjalung nation.*

Yaraando See *Dreaming tree of life.*

Yarra river and Port Phillip The *Koori* people have a story
about how the Yarra river and Port Phillip Bay, on which
Melbourne, the capital of Victoria, now stands, came about. The
area now known as Port Phillip Bay was once a flat plain and was
inhabited by the Bunurong, Kurung and Wathaurung people.
Inland lay a huge lake called Moorool. It covered much of the land
of the Wurundjeri people and an elder, Bar-wool, decided to drain
it. He began cutting a channel with a stone axe and cut a channel
to Port Phillip plain. The waters of Moorool rushed down and
flooded the land and the people living there had to flee to higher
ground.

There are other stories of the flooding of Port Phillip plain and
these stories may contain a continuous folk memory of the rising
of the seas at the end of the last ice age, thousands of years ago.

Another Koori story tells how one day, when the men were away
hunting and the women gathering roots and *yams*, some small
boys who were left behind began playing and upset a bucket of
water. This bucket was no ordinary bucket, but a magic one. Water
flooded out and flooded out and not only filled up the plain of
Port Phillip, but threatened to cover all the land. It was *Bunjil*,
Eaglehawk, who came to the rescue of the Kooris. He placed a
large rock on the Mornington peninsula and told the water to go
no further. Then he placed two huge rocks to make the heads
where the bay enters the sea. He told the water to flow between
them to enter the ocean.

See also *Crow.*

Yarrabah Yarrabah was a mission and now is an *Aboriginal* settlement near Cairns in Queensland where the Yidinyji and
Gungganyji people were concentrated by the invaders. Under a
succession of missionaries and government managers, their culture has been drastically changed, though cultural revitalization
movements keep some aspects alive.

See also *Gulibungay and his magic boomerang; Water sprites.*

Yayarr See *Pleiades*.

Yeddigee See *Dogs*.

Yellow ochre Yellow ochre in *Arnhem Land* is a sacred colour of the *Yiritja* moiety.
See also *Bark paintings; Red, black, yellow and white; Red ochre; White ochre*.

Yerrerdet-kurrk See *Murray river; Rigel*.

Yhi is the goddess of the *sun*. Yhi and *Biame* worked together in the creation of humankind.
See also *Marmoo*.

Yidaka See *Didjeridoo*.

Yirawala (1903–76) Yirawala was a famous painter who came from Kunwinjku (Croker Island) and has been called the *Aboriginal* Picasso. His bark paintings are dramatic compositions filled with motion and tension.
See also *Marwai the master painter*.

Yiritja (or Jiritja) is one of the two moieties of *Arnhem Land*. The main Yiritja cultural ancestors are *Barama and Laindjung*. Their sacred colour is *yellow ochre*.
See also *black; Duwa moiety; Gunabibi ceremonies; Nara; North-eastern Arnhem Land*.

Yolngu See *Arnhem Land; Barama and Laindjung myths; Djanggawul mythology and ceremonies; The Duwa moiety; North-eastern Arnhem Land; Rangga; Wangarr*.

Yothu Yindi Yothu Yindi are three Yulngu men from Yirrkala, *Arnhem Land*, Bakamana Yunupingu, Witiyana Mariko and Milkayngu Mununggurr, who formed the group Yothu Yindi to bring their music and dance to the rest of the world. They have been very successful at doing this and have toured extensively. They perform both traditional and contemporary music and dance and have had a song on the Top Forty hit parade in Australia and the United Kingdom.

Yowie See *Extinct giant marsupials*.

Yuedum See *Katatjuta*.

Yuendumu (Ngama Outcrop) Yuendumu is a Walbiri town which lies on the edge of the Tanami desert, north-west of Alice Springs. It and its sister town *Papunya* are famous as being the homes of the originators of the *Western Desert* style of dot painting. These paintings record the *Dreamings* of the Walbiri people in symbolic form.

There are many *rock paintings* here, the principal being one of the great snake *Jarapiri* stretched along a rock wall. Yuendumu is where Jarapiri, on his journey from Winbaraku, came up from the ground to teach the Walbiri the laws and customs which give shape to their lives. There is also a rock in the shape of Jarapiri's head pointing north to *Arnhem Land*, which is said to have been his ultimate destination.

See also *Dogs; Papunya Tula art*.

Yuggera people See *Mount Tabletop; Sleeping giant*.

Yugumbir people The Yugumbir people lived on the Logan river and they have preserved a full version of the mythology concerning the battle of the animals which marked the end of the *Dreamtime* and the reasons why it occurred in this area.

In the Dreamtime when many of the mountains were still being made, much anger was felt by the land animals against the sea animals who frequently made visits ashore. *Willy Wagtail* arranged a vast meeting of the land animals and birds at which it was decided to attack the sea animals next time they came ashore. It was decided to appoint the giant freshwater turtle Bingingerra to be the leader. In the ensuring battle the sea animals were driven back into the sea and never ventured on land again.

There were many casualties of the battle. Goanna suffered mortal wounds and crawled inland to the base of the Great Dividing Range and turned into rock, his body becoming Mount Maroon. *Koala* lost his tail in the fighting and was so upset that he climbed a tree where he makes his home to this day. He seldom comes down, lives on gum leaves and, when frightened, cries like a human baby. Blood Bird, or Mistletoe Bird, received his vivid red breast from fighting at the side of Turtle. Bingingerra, Turtle, carried the battle far out to sea and when it was over dragged his weary body back to shore and to the lagoons there. But he died

from his wounds and turned into stone, becoming Mount Bingingerra (Mt Witheren) which is in the shape of a giant turtle.
See also *Great battles; Uluru.*

Yukope the parakeet See *Bunjil.*

Yulunggul Yulunggul is the giant serpent which swallowed the Duwa *ancestral beings* the *Wawilag sisters* and then later regur gitated them. He is sometimes seen as a rainbow. He is said to make *lightning* with his forked tongue and the thunder is his voice.
See also *Duwa moiety; Gunabibi; Gunabibi ceremonies.*

Yuree See *Beehive.*

Yuru Ngawarla See *Adnyamathanha people.*

Yuwam the black snake See *Childbirth; Menstrual blood.*

Of further interest...

Dictionary of Mind, Body and Spirit

Eileen Campbell and J. H. Brennan

In our fast-changing world, many people are uneasy with the values that have grown out of a scientific, reductionist world view and are exploring different ideas and approaches. People are looking for answers to life's seemingly unanswerable questions. This dictionary will prove a useful starting-point. It covers a whole range of subjects—spiritual and esoteric traditions, paranormal phenomena, people and places—from acupressure to automatic writing, Spiritualism to Santeria, Zen to Zoroastrianism.

Eileen Campbell has studied with a variety of teachers from different religious traditions. In her work as a publisher she has been responsible for the publication of many important books dealing with spiritual growth and transformation. She has also compiled four anthologies: *A Dancing Star* (1991), *A Lively Flame* (1992), *The Unknown Region* (1993) and *A Fabulous Gift* (1994), all published by Aquarian.

J. H. Brennan is the author of many works on mind, body and spirit, including *Nostradamus, Visions of the Future* (Aquarian, 1992).

Dictionary for Dreamers

Over 500 archetypal symbols

Tom Chetwynd

Distilled from the collective wisdom of the great interpreters of dreams, this comprehensive key to the baffling language of dream symbolism is a thought-provoking and invaluable guide to the uncharted country of the mind. Tom Chetwynd has isolated for the first time the rich meanings of over 500 archetypal symbols from the indiscriminate mass of dream material, and rated the likelihoods of the various possible interpretations in each case. Here are the essential clues to understanding the ingeniously disguised, life-enriching, often urgent messages to be found in dreams.

'A thoughtful and sensible book, quite different from the usual dream book...fascinating.'
Manchester Evening News

'compulsive reading...marvellously imaginative'.
The Times

'...brings to bear both learning and insight. It should do much to open up new ground in the understanding of dream images.'
Prediction

Tom Chetwynd studied theology at London University, followed by many years' research into symbolism. The result was a three-volume work, comprising this book, *Dictionary of Sacred Myth* and *Dictionary of Symbols*.

Dictionary of Symbols

Tom Chetwynd

'Without symbols our lives would be as spiritually impoverished as sleep without dreams...'

Just as we dream every night without necessarily being aware of having dreamed, so our waking life is full of symbolism operating on an unconscious level. Drawn from the collective wisdom of the great psychologists, particularly Jung, this comprehensive and thought-provoking guide explains the language of symbols, Tom Chetwynd describes the major characteristics that recur in all symbolic material; identifying them can enable us to recognize the patterns and processes at work in our own minds, and to explore, develop and transform ourselves.

'A really remarkable book...written with a great deal of learning and good humour.'
Richard Holmes, *The Standard*

Dictionary of Sacred Myth

Tom Chetwynd

'There is only one symbolic language—and that is used by dreams, creative imagination, and myths.'

Myths depict the archetypal patterns in the drama of the psyche, the universal processes of life. The language of myths and dreams is simple and direct—but we have forgotten the art of interpreting it. In this fascinating compilation, Tom Chetwynd explores this oldest and most universal method of communication, drawing on the mythologies of the ancient world, Egypt, Classical Greece and Rome, as well as the insights of psychology and the mystical traditions of the world's religions.

As sacred myth is an attempt on the part of the human psyche to reflect the dynamics of the nature of the universe, so working with myths and symbols can bring renewed understanding of the ways of the soul.

Dictionary of Festivals

J. C. Cooper

Despite the great divides of continents and oceans, early civilizations were remarkably similar in their beliefs, inspired by common themes—birth and death, moon and sun, gods and heroes. Around the world man devised different ways of demonstrating corporate delight and thanks, hope and grief—through rituals, carnivals, fêtes, even sacrifice. This book brings together ceremonies and customs from both the oldest civilizations, including Babylonian, Chinese, Greek and Inca, and the major religions of today, including Hindu, Sikh, Hebrew and Christian.

The Dictionary of Festivals is a highly informative and accessible guide which takes us on a fascinating journey to every corner of the globe, describing in detail festivals ancient and modern, together with a variety of subjects associated with them and their performances. Placing emphasis on myth, religion and custom, J. C. Cooper's enlightening entries demonstrate how many of today's fairs, fêtes and holidays, so often taken for granted and associated with quite different occasions, are in fact direct descendants of rites and celebrations based on the primitive urges and instincts of ancient tribes and religions. Furthermore, this illustrated sourcebook will open up a world of forgotten feast days which people today can preserve for future generations.

DICTIONARY OF MIND, BODY AND SPIRIT	1 85538 328 4	£6.99	☐
DICTIONARY FOR DREAMERS	1 85538 295 4	£5.99	☐
DICTIONARY OF SYMBOLS	1 85538 296 2	£7.99	☐
DICTIONARY OF SACRED MYTH	1 85538 296 2	£5.99	☐

All these books are available from your local bookseller or can be ordered direct from the publishers.

To order direct just tick the titles you want and fill in the form below:

Name: _____

Address: _____

_____ Postcode: _____

Send to: Thorsons Mail Order, Dept 3, HarperCollins*Publishers*, Westerhill Road, Bishopbriggs, Glasgow G64 2QT.

Please enclose a cheque or postal order or your authority to debit your Visa/Access account—

Credit card no: _____

Expiry date: _____

Signature: _____

—to the value of the cover price plus:
UK & BFPO: Add £1.00 for the first book and 25p for each additional book ordered.
Overseas orders including Eire: Please add £2.95 service charge. Books will be sent by surface mail but quotes for airmail despatches will be given on request.

24 HOUR TELEPHONE ORDERING SERVICE FOR ACCESS/VISA CARDHOLDERS— **TEL: 0141 772 2281**